WAR AND ORDER:
REFLECTIONS ON
VIETNAM AND HISTORY

Studies in International Affairs Number 11

Studies in International Affairs Number 11

WAR AND ORDER: REFLECTIONS ON VIETNAM AND HISTORY

by George Liska

The Washington Center of Foreign Policy Research
School of Advanced International Studies
The Johns Hopkins University

The Johns Hopkins Press, Baltimore

FOREWORD

From the Spanish-American war to the war in Vietnam major changes in U.S. foreign policy have followed America's involvement in wars. In the cold war the Korean war was particularly fateful. It began the unforeseen extension of the policy of military containment to China and was followed by a marked expansion of American commitments and power in Asia. In this respect America's involvement in the Vietnamese war is a natural sequel to the Korean war.

All of America's previous military interventions in support of containment have led to expansions of American commitments. It is now widely assumed, however, that the war in Vietnam will lead to a contraction of American commitments—or at least to a reduction of the level of military and economic effort in support of them. The principal reason for this assumption is clear: the widespread feeling in the United States that the costs of this war became disproportionate to the purpose of fighting it and the prospect of winning it, and the consequent resolve to avoid direct participation in "national liberation wars" in the future. If the lesson of the war is that the United States must avoid involving its forces on the mainland of Asia and other regions of the world outside Europe, especially in wars that are partly internal, then it is logical that the United States should also avoid the political and military steps of containment that might lead to such involvements.

But this is not the only lesson and policy conclusion that one can reasonably draw from the war in Vietnam. Nor is the only alternative to retrenchment the continuation of containment according to the prevailing official American rationale, which seems to require virtually automatic intervention against communist incursions on the grounds that small aggressions, if left unpunished, must lead to larger aggressions and World War III. Another policy and rationale, as different from undiscriminating "globalism" as from "neo isolationism," can be constructed on the conception of the United States as an imperial but nonimperialistic state with such extensive power that its vital interests should be defined in terms of elementary international order and its power should be directed toward maintaining such order. This is a conception that has attracted growing attention both in the United States and western Europe. An earlier booklet in this series by Professor Liska, *Imperial America*, contributed a broad historical perspective to this awareness.

This current essay elaborates the imperial conception, refines the scope and limits of its practical application, and relates it more specifically to America's involvement in the Vietnamese war. It is not a prescription for conducting that war but a concept of American policy and role that tries to place the war in proper perspective, so that, whatever its outcome may be, the lessons that we draw from it may be more pertinent to the future than momentary reactions.

vi

For a comparable effort to place the war in perspective, which reaches fundamentally different
conclusions, readers are referred to Robert W.
Tucker, *Nation or Empire? The Debate over American Foreign Policy*, number 10 in this series.

June, 1968   ROBERT E. OSGOOD
                                        Director
                                        Washington Center of
                                        Foreign Policy Research

AUTHOR'S PREFACE

The purpose of this essay is to present one possible perspective—that of world order—in which to view the present American ordeal in Asia. Within the general consensus on American purposes in the world there are three basic objections to United States' global involvement as currently dramatized by the war in Vietnam. I have devoted a chapter to each of them.

The first objection is that United States' global interventionism is contrary to the unique genius of the nation as expressed in its domestic traditions and the best of its foreign policy tradition (with the exception of the aberrant pursuit of "manifest destiny" at the turn of the century). Those who argue this position claim that it would be disastrous for the United States to follow in the path of other once powerful nations and to yield to the temptations of power and its arrogant exercise. An attempt to present a less self-centered view of American foreign policy is made in the first chapter.

The second objection is that in the nuclear age, more than ever before, global interventionism is counterproductive because it generates conflict and involvement in conflict. The argument is that conflicts must be avoided because they are too dangerous and prone to escalation, and that they can be avoided because nuclear weapons plus other transformations in the international environment generate both a presumption against the use of force and alternatives to it. This set of propositions is discussed in the second chapter.

The third basic objection is that U.S. interventions around the world represent an outdated anticommunism, sometimes disguised by references to world order and American responsibilities. The critics maintain that once foreign policy is freed from this obsession, it would become much easier to restrict the scope of interventions, to select the few occasions of disorder that constitute a threat to national security and therefore justify intervention, and to transfer most tasks of order-maintenance to local powers or multilateral arrangements.

The issue of order and its maintenance is discussed in the third chapter. The discussion carries over into the fourth chapter, which concentrates directly on the debate over Vietnam. Chapter IV will offend some in that positions and premises are here reformulated in terms of logical antithesis rather than in specific terms that can be attributed to individual disputants. The anti-interventionist position is defined by contrast with my own, which is interventionist. The essay concludes on a questioning note regarding American purpose and destiny. The United States is a pluralistic, multiracial society that is presently casting about for domestic equilibrium and social justice. The question is whether it will conduct this internal quest in retreat from, or with continuing and deepening involvement in, a world society that is confronting the same problems.

War and Order is a companion piece to *Imperial America*, an earlier publication in this series. It deals with individual facets of the problem of imperial order and role which the former essay ignored or treated tangentially. Both little books were seen through editorially by John Gallman, the Washington Editor of The Johns Hopkins Press, with a dedication matched only by his disagreement with my bias. It is to him and readers like him, willing to bestow time and attention on uncongenial views, that I dedicate the pages that follow.

CONTENTS

   I. The Conquest of the United States by
      History   1

  II. Recurrent Conflicts and Alternative Order   15

 III. Elementary Order and Pre-eminent Power   46

 IV. Anti-Interventionism and Imperial Con-
      sciousness   81

  V. Conclusion   111

I. THE CONQUEST OF THE UNITED STATES BY HISTORY

The foreign policy of the United States is surrounded by question marks. So must be any discussion of it. Is America already, or ought she become, an imperial power—a power in quest not of colonies or neocolonial sway, but of international order, and of national integrity as distinct from territorial security? Should the United States cease being the greatest world power and settle for being "little America" even before it has proved itself to possess the stuff of either a great society or a great nation? Should it retrench commitments and interests and retreat to the doubtfully protective shelter of multilateralism? These are the questions of the day, as Americans face a combined crisis at home and abroad.

Put more searchingly, what is the innermost drive behind American action abroad at this critical juncture? Is the United States passing through another transient spell of imperialism in a wrongheaded pursuit of a myth of destiny? If so, external hindrances and internal frustrations will easily blunt a zeal without legitimate purpose.

Or is the United States caught between its desire to extend abroad the balanced pluralism of the domestic polity and the reality of an imbalanced international system characterized by American preponderance and by a host of smaller states vying for local preponderance? If this is so, then the U.S. balance-of-power policy, I shall argue, cannot but assume the outward forms and purposes of an imperial policy for order. In this case, opponents of the involvement in Vietnam have deluded themselves, as have some of its defenders, by treating the crisis as a one-time, not-to-be-repeated deviation from America's basically noninterventionist stance.

Or thirdly, does an overactive American foreign policy merely project abroad internal social maladjustments aggravated by derangement in the constitutional balance of executive and legislative powers? A fitful, compulsive external activism can signal an incipient drift into decline and merge with defensive reactions to it. If so, then both critics and defenders of the Vietnamese war have missed the point by addressing themselves to the American society as one capable of making choices, defining external responsibilities, and harmonizing internal and external problems and needs.

The three alternative orientations of American policy are analogous to those of major European nations in the past. There is a prevalent tendency to regard any similarity between American and other foreign policies as fortuitous and superficial. The same school of thought regards any possible continuity between traditional and contemporary international politics in the same light. In this view, even if there were a powerful trend toward international politics as usual, the United States is not a nation to submit to such a trend, since it is unique in its origins and character. Instead, the United States ought to exercise its genius and power to uphold its uniqueness and impress it, without imposing it, upon the international system with which it is linked. The United States, like so many others before it, must not ascend the dreary steps from parochialism to empire only to find at the end the god-decreed penalty for hubris. Rather, it should set out to save the world by the power of example, eschewing the one thing denied humans: an exemplary exercise of power. Too strong and not meek enough to be the Christ among nations, the United States should still bend all its efforts to live up to the Sermon on the Mount within its borders, and having done so, conquer all that is conquerable by the spirit. The peace of justice, the argument concludes, is at once more stable and more noble than yet another facsimile of the *Pax Romana*.

I shall pass over the moral presumptuousness of such a sense of national uniqueness and stress, instead, its superficial side. My argument is simple. American foreign policy has conformed to the evolutionary pattern of other major nations as the United States has moved from the favored conditions surrounding its origins into the full complexity of mature international life. Only a home-bound historiography, lacking in sympathetic understanding of the foreign policy predicaments of other (especially European) nations, can hold otherwise. Only such a self-centered outlook can continue to perceive the sweep of American foreign policy as categorically different from that of, say, Spain, France, or Britain, the other nations which at one point or another aspired to the privilege and submitted to the exigencies of paramount power.

It may be difficult to equate the ideas and ideologies underlying the Cortés of Castile and the U.S. Congress, the Crown of Rheims and the Constitution of Philadelphia, or even the Magna Carta and the Bill of Rights. It may be equally hazardous to compare the personal world-views of a Thomas Jefferson and a Philippe-Auguste, of a Clive and a Clay, or of a Medina Sidonia and a George Marshall, who, following upon the consolidators and the expansionists, wielded their sovereign's sword at crucial moments between supremacy and a balance of power. But it is possible to place in a single perspective the parallel sweep of the foreign policies of great nations in the proper temporal sequences. In such a perspective American foreign policy can be viewed as going through certain typical phases which, with an acceptable degree of interpretive distortion and actual discontinuities, marked other nations' policies in comparable international conditions. Similarities in over-all development and dynamic then appear as more significant than the peculiarities of situation and style.

I can only suggest here what I have in mind. American foreign policy was conceived in an expansive mood even before the nation achieved independence; the mood was typified by Benjamin Franklin and his vision of a North American empire first within, and then outside, the larger British empire. Thus, too, the insufficient power and the grand vision of England's Plantagenet kings strained toward an Angevin empire comprising the crown of France. France herself was inspired by the crusading spirit of a saintly Capetian, and what was to become Spain provided an underpinning for the volatile Moor. Such expansiveness seems to characterize the earliest phase of a nation and its policy. In this phase a transcendent sanction, be it that of Chivalry, Faith, or indefeasible hereditary Right, assures even a shifting and often divided authority of the indispensable degree of domestic order. And if the state is a charter member of a likewise nascent international system, a weakly structured, unarticulated, permissive field of external forces is apt to constitute a lure rather than a restraint to expansion. The resulting early drives into the realms of force and fancy will, however, tend to peter out and then result in the first spell of sobriety.

The next phase is no longer one of nervous expansiveness but of physical consolidation. Policy is now more or less systematically and consciously directed toward securing the state's territory within a natural compass and a viable habitat. Here belong the foreign policies of the later Capetian and the early Valois Kings, husbanding their strength and enlarging the royal domain so that "Feudalism" would come to be synonymous with "France"; the policies of the early Tudors, transferring emphasis from the conquest of France to that of Wales and Scotland; and those of the Catholic Kings, combining Castile and Aragon into a base for the reconquest of Spain. This was likewise the phase during which the United States spread out step by step southward and westward on the continent. At this stage an increasingly monopolistic wielder of foreign-policy authority will involve himself in remote issues only, if at all, to increase and profit from the inhibitions besetting other powers. He will seek and find closer at hand the opportunity and the strength for solid achievement. America's immunity to outside interference in this phase was unique in degree but not in kind; in her case, too, immunity was the result of the reciprocally stalemated, limited reach and opportunistic reactions of potentially hostile (European) powers within her zone of consolidation.

These two aspects of the formative period—expansion and consolidation—tend to overlap. They correspond to the twin drive of a developing organism for self-affirmation in gesture and self-realization in growth. By contrast, the phase immediately following consolidation, that of exuberance, stands out clearly by itself. Exuberance is the common denominator of apparently unrelated external activity. Examples are the drive of the new French monarchy, released from the Anglo-Burgundian threat, into Italy; the drives of the Conquistadors for a New Spain and of the Elizabethans for a New England; and the drive which propelled the new-formed power of America into the Caribbean and the Pacific, marking what a critic called at the time the conquest of the United States by Spain. At this stage, individual and group energies overflow the home base and are channeled into the low-pressure areas of the international system—areas which for the last two of the European powers and the United States lay outside the respective continents. The internal side effect is to reduce the threat to stability owing to an excess of political talent and ambition which, if bottled up and soured, would tend to endanger a smooth progress toward the next phase.

Exuberance has a way of feeding upon itself before it reaches the point of its own negation. States bound to and bounded by territory are not knights careening off toward ever-receding horizons, at least not for long. Charles VIII of France, any more than Charles XII of Sweden, is not history's idea of a responsible steward. Self-aggrandizement will sooner or later be tempered by self-limitation. This may result in the nation's progress toward the maturity of managing the field of external forces in the direction of balance or, if national resources were too severely depleted in the expansionist period (witness Portugal and Sweden), the result is apt to be drift toward self-isolation.

The no-man's land between exuberance and maturity is the locus of the greatest ambiguity in statecraft and the terrain for the most intriguing controversies. I refer to the two faces of a single phase of policy development: one is the disciplined drive for superior power; the other is the acceptance and cultivation of balance. The first may occur in the interest of primacy, world order, pre-emptive self-defense, commercial profit, or, underlying all the others, self-assertive prestige. The balance of power facet may not visibly differ from the first, especially when quest for equilibrium unfolds against the background of a recently experienced external threat. The policy of the balance of power will manifest itself in the pursuit of a favorable balance which the subject of the policy will identify with justice and its object with hegemony. Here belongs the foreign policy of Habsburg Spain in association with the Holy Roman Empire before and after the climactic efforts and defeats of, first, Charles V, and, second, Philip II. The aggregate Catholic Habsburg power felt threatened in the one and only Faith as well as the unity of Nation and Empire and was defied from the outside by both fearful and cynical France and both fearful and greedy England; it sought alternately a higher order in supremacy and an irreducible condition of existence in balance. Here, too, belongs the foreign policy of France beginning with Henry IV and Cardinal Richelieu, reacting to the trauma of Habsburg encirclement and reaching the high watermark of driving power with Louis XIV. Last but not least, England, too, occupied this phase in the period beginning with the first of the modern continental kings (William III, the Dutchman). Her reaction was to the irritations produced by French arrogance; the high watermark of her dominant if often dissimulated power was reached when the fall of Napoleon accelerated the decline of France.

This same, the present, phase of American foreign policy began in two instalments, identified with the first and the second Roosevelt. It was exacerbated by the Soviet threat. And it has now reached its high watermark in the wake of the threat's recession and the reappearance (or, some would say, invention) of yet another challenge from Communist China. America's drive for a "just balance" combines within its protean compass the transcendent rationale of imperial Spain (replacing faith with freedom), the driving restlessness and chronic insecurity of France, and England's domestically induced and temperamentally conditioned hesitancies and concealments. It differs from the others in that it may still achieve what it set out to accomplish.

In this phase of maturity, foreign policy will be typically underpinned by relatively ample resources. More essential still, the resources will be elastic in the sense of being readily mobilized and augmented for the purpose of either sustaining self-assertion or containing expansion. The politics of coalition characteristic of balance-of-power policies will be facilitated if a correspondingly matured international system is comprised of increasingly diversified states —ascendant, stabilized, and declining—with both dynamic and relatively static domestic politics and foreign policies. This was the case for the European system beginning at least with the seventeenth century. That the global system of today has not yet achieved this degree of maturity is the second main reason (next to Soviet rivalry) why America's pursuit of balance has tended to propel her toward preponderance.

The direct line from exuberance, we have noted, is toward a disciplined assertion of power and its restraint, the two interdependent sides of self-assured and realistic statecraft. The line from maturity would then seem to be, in the normal course of events, toward decline, characterized by compulsive attempts to avert or forestall it. To this compulsive foreign-policy phase belong Spain under the later Philips, whose desperate efforts to renew grandeur in alliance with Austria culminated in the Thirty Years' war; the French Revolutionary and Napoleonic phoenix, rising from the ashes of the dynastic statecraft of the *ancien régime*; and the Second Empire of Victorian, or Social Darwinian, England, doomed to go down in yet another war fought over thirty years in two parts.

The compulsive phase is the most strident one. A leading man, movement, or party will pursue the paramount objective of spectacular success in the external domain, which appears more malleable than the domestic one. In this phase, there is increasingly little congruence between the national system and policy and the international system, as ever more newcomers supplement and partly supplant the original, founding members of the system—be it the European or the present global system. But this very fluidity creates a hospitable environment for compulsive foreign policy, inasmuch as resistance to it will appear to be reduced by the existence of powers yet more decayed or not yet quite formed.

The most conspicuous example of compulsive foreign policy has been that of Hitler's Germany—a country whose internal development lagged behind that of the environing international system to the detriment of both, creating a derangement which was finally expressed by Germany's reaching out for an imperial role at a time when Europe as a system neither wanted nor needed the role's exercise by any one of its members. To the extent that the United States is being propelled presently toward an imperial role in the global system, it does so in response to the system's needs rather than its internal strains. This in itself, apart from other indices, suggests that this country has not entered upon the phase of compulsive expansionism. There may be elements of decay appearing in the American body politic. But, if doubt can be entertained as to the position of the United States on the developmental spectrum, it is largely owing to a different factor: the recurrence of an impulse to withdraw, an impulse elevated to a permanent posture in the foreign policy phase which normally follows the compulsive phase.

For the United States to retrench drastically its international activities at this stage would be at best premature. It is not likely. Like individuals, so nations worthy of the name will not withdraw into repose in their external dealings and thus, almost inevitably, submit to the momentum of decline, until they have explored in action the outermost limits of possible achievement. Spain did not withdraw before that happened and neither did France nor Britain. We hear much today of America's overextension, requiring retrenchment as a matter of both sound sense and social health. Yet no one can say what is "overextension" until a nation has been forced into restricting the radius of its action by a whole series of increasingly serious frustrations. As we move from antiquity to modern times, it is ever less convincing to regard great states as having declined because they overtaxed their resources. The last core-state of an empire to which the verdict can be at all plausibly applied is Spain and, more specifically, Castile, because of the peculiar makeup of her material power. England, Spain, and France, in a descending order, built their greatness on efforts way beyond their parochial frontiers. Their positions abroad held them above or on a par with rival nations with superior indigenous power, not least in terms of territory and population: France in the case of England and Spain, and Germany in the case of France and England. They declined as a result of desperate efforts to fend off such immediate and stronger adversaries with the aid of resources from their remote holdings, not as a result of attempts to cling to such holdings. Indeed, in the case of all three, to different degrees, efforts and achievements far from home helped build or rebuild the nation's solidarity and self-confidence in hours of internal distress or external defeat. Conversely, when remote assets and obligations were amputated, this provided only temporary relief, if any, as demoralization and resulting strains undermined the once imperial body politic itself.

A major question about a protracted war far from the American homeland is whether it warrants a Great Debate. In the history of the United States such debates have been exercises in internal persuasion substituting for the lasting instructive shock of foreign invasion, which has fixed the position and course of less fortunate nations. Has the United

States reached a point of fundamental decision comparable to the decision between isolationism and internationalism that was made in the First World War and confirmed in the Second? Or is the debate over Vietnam to be compared with the debate over permanent stationing of troops in Europe after World War II, bearing not so much on two different fundamental options as on the implementation of an orientation already established? If it is the first, if it concerns a decision between a new, embittered internationalism and a new, self-confident but self-restrained, imperialism, who will define the issues? Life or theory; elected leaders or their critics; the Democratic or the Republican Party? What will be the political cost of launching a new definition of the national purpose which might prove lastingly unpopular as compared with the cost of adhering to proven but tired rationalizations?

In another century, an intermittent debate similar to the one now rocking America absorbed much of the best of the political talent in Great Britain. The issue was active involvement on the continent and overseas. The arguments against involvement were strikingly similar to those used today (even more so than the arguments for involvement, which have since shed much of the nineteenth-century ideological trappings). The Liberal-Radical proponents of noninvolvement, while differing in the manner and intensity of their opposition, all fought to prevent Britain from being the "knight errant of the human race," except perhaps when she would charge against their own pet enemy. They preferred to depend on the protection of the British navy and wished to avoid indirectly benefiting another power, be it France or Russia, by futile British initiatives.

They wished to spare Britain the domestic social consequences of foreign intervention against a revolutionary power (France) in the wars of the Revolution and Napoleon and the external frustrations of intervention against reactionary (Russian) power in the Crimean war. They alternately decried the balance of power and glorified the concert of the powers. They wanted the House of Commons, on behalf of the people, to determine foreign policy over and against the executive branch of government. They pilloried obscure governmental commitments after these turned out to generate later entanglements (in the Eastern Question in the 1870s), while excoriating obscure private interests as the guilty party if involvement occurred without prior official commitments (in South Africa).

The consequences of the Radicals' agitation were often contrary to their wish both in Europe and overseas. Their moral victory in Parliament for nonintervention in 1850 (in the aftermath of the Don Pacifico affair, which produced Palmerston's intervention against Greece) did not prevent public opinion from desiring intervention on a bigger issue in 1853 (against Russia, which culminated in the Crimean war) to make up for Britain's tolerating Russian repressions in Hungary in 1849. A more lasting spell of British nonintervention in Europe started in 1864. It came to foster diplomatic dependence on Germany after 1870. The resulting German conceit, however, merely nourished the conditions necessitating reinvolvement against Germany in the twentieth century. In the colonial sphere, opposition to the Boer war stopped short of the Radicals' working for Boer victory. Instead, they were reduced to agitating against the conduct of the war and in favor of a change of heart in Britain leading to negotiations which would reconcile presumably reconcilable interests.

The Boer war discredited the British imperialists even more than it confounded their domestic opponents. It did so not only because the war stood for a questionable exercise of the imperial role, but also because it coincided with the waning of British imperial power.

The recurrence of arguments does not prove them right or wrong; it merely indicates that an argument is not original and the underlying events are not unique. The British Radicals failed on the whole to control British foreign policy on the issues which interested them most as moralists. They were repeatedly reduced to wondering at the defection of their leaders to a power policy abroad once in power at home—at a Gladstone being "sucked" into Egypt just as a Johnson has allegedly been sucked into Vietnam. They could console themselves with the thought that power corrupts. But they rarely paused to ask whether, perhaps, foreign issues are better surveyed from the heights of responsibility than from the hollows of dissent; whether, useful as it is to oppose the complacency of government at home, Radical political intelligence may not end at the water's edge. It is a poor consolation and a debatable proposition to say that the British Radicals have been proven right posthumously.[1] It may be more accurate to say that they have been proven right for a Britain which they might neither recognize as the fulfillment of their dream nor approve as the dream's approximation.

[1] As Professor A. J. P. Taylor argues in *The Troublemakers* (Bloomington, Ind.: Indiana University Press, 1958), which I have drawn on for the British data.

II. RECURRENT CONFLICTS AND ALTERNATIVE ORDERS

The imperial role of the United States should be perceived as a consequence of two converging conditions. On the one hand, we have the mature state of American foreign policy in its present phase, which is characterized by tension between a concern with the balance of power and an inclination toward supremacy. On the other hand, we have the present state of the international system, where there is the need for a modicum of order, if only as a condition of orderly long-term internal developments in critical countries, including the United States. The emphasis in evaluating the imperial role can be on the subjective aspect, stressing the actor's readiness or propensity to act expansively in terms of power, or it can be on the objective aspect, stressing the conditions of order and asserting responsibility. The emphasis is crucial, since it will influence or even determine one's attitude toward the involvement of the United States in military conflict. Such involvement is the unavoidable consequence of any but a parasitic or formal participation (be it exploitative, auxiliary, mediatory, or institutional) in much of contemporary international politics.

Conflict is still the distinctive feature of international politics outside the developed states of Europe and Japan, which are either temporarily exhausted and demoralized or perhaps lastingly reformed. In the vaster unreclaimed areas, rampant with unsatisfied grievances, the choice is one between structured conflict and unstructured chaos. In practice this means that interventions may use and oppose violence at different levels of deployment, utilizing different kinds of force. It also means that interventions may occur at different stages of both the disintegration of existing order and the expansion of forces and powers committed to another vision of eventual order. In simpler terms, this means that a salient power like the United States is rather restricted in its options. It can choose to fight important but still limited engagements, such as that in Vietnam, at a relatively early stage of dislocation in the regional structure of power and will. Or it can choose to retrench until such time as it may have to fight a bigger war or face more diffuse and even less coercible elements of disorder under still less favorable conditions. The United States chose to fight in Vietnam while there was still an authority that was willing to supply manpower, a battleground, and a rationale for the contest. It avoided the risk of having to fight later in conditions of spreading subversion by some and self-protective effacement by others, on the mainland and possibly in the island realms of Asia.

The essence of the anti-interventionist or anti-imperial position is to deny the dangers of inaction, while interventionists are inclined to favor timely action even against "hypothetical" dangers. One side believes in the automatic erosion (by local developments) and reciprocal paralysis (by conflicting ambitions and aspirations) of actual or potential threats—Chinese, North Vietnamese, communist, or other—before they reach the point of clearly endangering the national security of the United States. The other side gives higher credence to the probability, given the distribution of power and will in the world generally and in Asia particularly, of a snow-balling momentum of unchecked hostile forces—deemed disordering from the American perspective—and of supine or submissive local responses to them.

The accuracy of the more pessimistic view cannot be convincingly established even in retrospect if it is acted upon. All one can say for pessimism about the predicament of men and states is that it forms the basis of the traditional approach to statecraft. Only the pessimistic approach has been tested historically, and those adhering to it have usually been successful in averting the particular age's idea of supreme evil, even if often at considerable cost. To take the more pessimistic position, to act to avert possible catastrophe where there might have been only the annoyance of local turbulence and intermittent terror, is to come to terms with a dreary prospect for this country: recurrent American use of force, even if, one may hope, in a more limited and manageable form than in Vietnam. Before deciding whether this prospect is tolerable, let us first look at the problem of conflict a little more closely. Then, after a review of feasible types of international order, we shall examine the elements of continuity and the conditions of possible change in international relations.

If participation in conflict is to be truly discretionary, the incidence of force must be shown to vary as a function of good intentions and prudent policies. The facts of the matter do not clearly support this particular kind of human omnipotence in international politics. The rough impression emerging from history is of a relatively constant sum of used force in different periods that are sufficiently short to be significant for an individual lifetime. Such a diagnosis, if correct, makes the use of force by the United States more acceptable. If conflict is inherent in any period of international politics, and if there is no sure way to escape from it, it makes sense for a major country to control the scale and distribution of conflict by timely engagement. Provided that the ordering power learns how to endure recurrent conflicts, the tendency for the sum of conflict to remain constant will save it from being overwhelmed by too many concurrent engagements.

The impression of a fixed sum of conflict over time emerges from both of the ready sources of insight: sweeping historical contemplation and more minute analysis of the time one lives in, in our case the period after World War II. In the experience of the European state system, once use of force ceased to be virtually continuous, relative quiet tended to follow upon major conflicts, which had exhausted the capabilities of the belligerents and the capacity of the system of states as a whole to absorb conflict and avoid collapse. If this meant that major conflict would periodically subside, it also meant that it would not completely disappear. Major protracted conflicts tended to abate only as they were being replaced by an emerging conflict, in an often lengthy process of gradual supersession rather than in sudden and dramatic suppression. It is as if the system of states, unable to assimilate too much conflict at any one time, could not properly function for any length of time without some conflict. Peripheral military engagements would normally take up at least part of the slack, as it were, in periods of relative quiet on the central fronts. It is one thing to exceed the limit of the system's absorptive capacity for war and destruction; it is quite another to allow the capabilities which help keep the system in being to atrophy through protracted disuse.

To illustrate briefly, the conflict between the Christian and Moslem worlds faded away only with the rise of conflicts among individual Christian and Moslem powers; the struggle between Bourbon and Habsburg with the rise of the parallel and related Anglo-French and Austro-Prussian contests; the rivalry between England and Russia with the rise of the conflict of both with Germany. Only minor, peripheral, or colonial conflicts existed in the long periods of peace at the beginning of all three of the "modern" centuries starting with the eighteenth, most conspicuously in the relatively long spells of partial peace among the great powers in the nineteenth century.

What do we see in the period following World War II? First, we see the progressive accentuation of organized interstate violence in the world at large beginning in 1956, after the period of abstinence in the late 1940s and early 1950s (if we treat the Korean "miscalculation" as an exception). In these years, the tolerance for force in a war-weary system was largely filled by intracountry violence of the guerrilla kind, from Greece to Malaya. Second, we see the subsidence of the Soviet-American conflict concurrently with the rise of the two powers' antagonism with China; we see the difficulty to maintain simultaneously both the East-West and the South-North contest (unless both should converge in Sino-American hostility). We can also envisage the probability that a decline in conflict between organized armed forces of considerable magnitude, perhaps following upon the end of the war in Vietnam, will be accompanied by increased incidence of quasiwars between weak states or by even less-structured forms of group violence. Such lower forms of force are not necessarily stimulated by the misbehavior of greater powers. They may instead be held in abeyance or moderated by concern over the tensions and dangers created by the larger conflict. The fighting between India and Pakistan was not resumed, the Arab-Israeli war was not prolonged or expanded, and Indonesia did not intensify its confrontation with Malaysia—quite the contrary—while the war in Vietnam increased in intensity. Nigeria was left alone to enact and perhaps adjust its inner turmoil while Communist China was compelled by the adjoining Vietnam conflict to impose a ceiling on permissible internal violence.

There is another point to be made, bearing on still shorter time spans. It would seem to confirm the twin principle of a constant sum of conflict over time and of a maximum of assimilable amount of conflict at any one time in a semi-ordered system of states. Even at the peak of the cold war there were never two intense military crises unfolding between the superpowers at one time, and for good reason. The Soviet Union, rather than trying to scatter the attention and the resources of the United States in all corners of the world, studiously avoided overstraining both resources and attention so as not to force the United States to seek deliverance from many irritating conflicts in one supreme confrontation. Acute tension in Europe, such as the first or the second Berlin crisis, did not coincide with the fighting in Asia or with a really tense confrontation in the Middle East or the Caribbean. In Asia proper, crisis over Laos preceded (and may follow) that over Vietnam, but did not parallel it. When in the Pueblo crisis a small and extremist communist country, North Korea, risked breaking the rules at the height of the Vietnamese war, the existing degree of Soviet influence was apparently exercised in favor of caution, while the United States—finding itself in a forward posture—shrank from adding a conflict with North Korea to that with North Vietnam.

Quite apart from communist prudence, the reason for conflict-rationing lies in the present global system itself. Although vast in geographic compass, the system is poor both in usable power and in the numbers of states able to employ power with more than parochial and passing effect. The system lacks sufficient potential in actors, attention, and alignment alternatives to enable it at any one time to comprise or tolerate several acute interstate conflicts with mutually exclusive requirements and implications. Neither the Soviet Union nor the United States can muster enough allies, energy, and subtlety to pursue, actively and simultaneously, the conflict with one another and with China as long as China refuses to identify with either. India cannot with significant effect both head a coalition of the less-developed "South" against one or both of the industrialized superpowers and concurrently depend on them for defense of her northern border (since there is no alternative southern power who could help her).

By contrast, after a period of relative international calm, conflict will intensify. It will be stimulated, for example, by the recovered possibility of surprise; the difficulty to estimate correctly the relative power and readiness for action of the adversary; or by the possibility to attract allies by misrepresenting the adversary's capabilities or will. Authentic error may lead to war by miscalculation, whereas simulated error may produce a revolution by misrepresentation. The Soviet Union came to grief over the first in Korea; Peking and Hanoi now hope to attain success by means of the second.

Default in Vietnam would not necessarily lead to a third world war in full nuclear panoply by encouraging great-power aggressors. It might, as we shall later argue, only increase the tendency to fall back upon nuclear weapons as the only efficient defense against the other modern form of unorthodox violence. But a premature termination of the war would almost certainly create a vacuum of organized and controlled conflict as well as authority in the state system. Such a vacuum might set the stage not so much for wars like those that attended Germany's bid for hegemony but for a chaotic interregnum comparable to the period following Rome's descent from empire.

There are various types of world order, roughly characterized by the restraint exercised by the *potential* perpetrator of violence and other parties. There are also various types of disorder, roughly defined by the degree of control exercised over violence by its *actual* perpetrator. I shall discuss first the types of order and then those of disorder.

Five kinds of broadly defined world order seem particularly salient. These vary in structure according to the degree of concentration or diffusion of authority. They vary in the degree to which they would effect restraint by means of an ordering authority, by reciprocal restraint between adversaries, or by self-restraint of potential disturbers—a self-restraint which is a function of capacity and compulsion to anticipate responses to actions inimical to order or justice as understood at the time. The different orders may also vary in the degree to which they are suited to contend with disorder resulting from the interaction of states and with internal disorder resulting from overreaction to galling conditions or inadequate governments. Moreover, each type of order will differ over time in the degree to which it is supported as desirable or accepted as legitimate, not necessarily because it is supremely just or efficacious but because it is superior to available alternatives.

The first kind of world order, in both age and simplicity, is imperial. It is defined by the existence of a materially or culturally preponderant power—ancient Egypt in the Eastern Mediterranean world, Rome throughout the Mediterranean, China in her orbit, which at times encompassed both Korea and Vietnam. Imperial order rests on the fear or respect of lesser powers, secured and held by the judicious alternation of forcefulness, self-restraint, and munificence of the imperial state. In the newer age, we know only the contested pretensions and partial realizations of the imperial role of the Holy Roman Empire under Charles V, France under Louis XIV and Napoleon, and Great Britain under Lords Palmerston and Beaconsfield. Even a contested superiority of power can, however, produce order more successfully and more peacefully than a delicate balance of power. The one condition is that the primary power's self-restraint be allowed to follow its self-aggrandizement—a rare tolerance which explains why there has been a British peace but, on the part of the great continental states, only short-lived supremacies.

The newer age is replete with cases of a second kind of order, defined by contest over primacy between two or (rarely) more aspirants to the imperial function. We call these contests hegemonic. In modern history they pitted against one another very different powers in a very similar manner—the Habsburgs of Spain and Austria against the Valois and Bourbons of France; continental-maritime France against maritime-continental England; Tsarist Russia and Imperial Germany against Parliamentary Britain; the private-capitalistic United States against the state-capitalistic Soviet Union. This type of order is very common for the Occident. Elementary order is extracted from the combination of self-restraint and reciprocal restraint imposed on the principal parties by the closeness of the contest and the consequent regard for the self-assertion of third states in behalf of their interests. It will be a matter of momentary fashion whether this interest is asserted in the name of peace, order, development, or equilibrium.

The third kind of order consists of the deliberate or unwitting checks of a balance of power. Such a balance may be fitfully institutionalized in a concert. It is served by the existence of several equal or near-equal powers, and may usefully revolve around a conservative "first (power) among equals" which loosely manages the system without dominating it and controls the whole without coercing its parts.

The later eighteenth and nineteenth centuries provide the only well-known examples of a balance-of-power order. In this type of order, external restraint becomes anticipatory self-restraint when first military and then diplomatic moves of the other great powers become predictable. Individual self-restraint becomes collective great power order when it undergirds authority over lesser states. This will happen when the utility of smaller states in the still ongoing but greatly muted great power competition becomes negligible enough to make them less valuable as allies in contests than they are as objects of cooperation. This type of order has recently attained great appeal and favor, despite its present inapplicability in the most critical parts of the world.

The fourth type of order is one flowing from restraints institutionalized in a world organization such as the United Nations. Such an organization is at once more and less than an order rooted only in the contingent exercise of controlling or countervailing power. It will, we now know, fluctuate in efficacy depending on momentary constellations of power and the interests and needs of the national members. It may never die, but it may also never grow up to assume any permanent or reliable significant function, as both the Middle Eastern and the Far Eastern crises have demonstrated. Only a superhumanly provident imperial power might launch a global international security organization into self-sustaining collective authority that could restrain the several members. International organization might then be the residuary legatee of one, noncolonial, imperial state rather than a legatee of many colonial empires (as it once was thought). It might receive and fulfill one general mandate rather than dissipate its feeble powers in an attempt to exercise many.

The fifth and last possibility is the total absence of centrally ordering power or centrally converging power relationships. Pockets of local order in a sea of disorder would mark an interregnum between any two of the above types of order. Anarchy and chaos would blight the spirit while fresh power for a new order would invisibly take shape under cover of sterile conflict.

The choice between the kinds of order outlined above can be stated more briefly and simply than the alternatives. The imperial option now seems possible. The world system is again rudimentary, when seen for a moment apart from its sustaining armature of the Soviet-American conflict and American commitment and power. In consequence, analogies with the state systems of antiquity are more revealing than analogies with the state system of the *ancien régime*. In addition, the imperial option seems preferable to the second type of order, which results from Russia's contention for primacy with China or from China's and Russia's separate or joint struggle with the United States. Imperial order also appears more realistic and feasible than the third or balance-of-power order. Such order is presently inconceivable in areas outside Europe, and even for Europe a balance of power would depend on a vigilant and tolerant exercise of America's over-all global primacy. As for the fourth and fifth extreme possibilities, world government and regionalized interregnum, the first may be dismissed as utopian; the second, because it is nightmarish.

To accept an imperial role for the United States is to make proper adjustments in one's view of the present era's dominant conflict. In a world seen as bipolar, the principal function of the United States was (and may again become) to contain the Soviet

Union or its successor to the role of the challenger. In a world seen as having a single focus in America's salient power, the key preoccupation and related American function has to do with a growing number of more varied threats.

The containment of the more assertive of the communist great powers is still necessary; but it may well be secondary to the containment of disorder caused ultimately by some form of insufficient power. Despite the nonfulfillment of the key expectation underlying the cold war—the ability of the Soviets to move toward material parity—the Soviet Union will go on trying to improve its position relative to the United States. It will stage comebacks as a global competitor from an improved position in nuclear deterrence and respectable diplomacy. It may even improve its conventional military resources, which are required for sustained intervention in areas remote from the home base. The best prospects for Soviet achievements would seem to be in Europe and in areas contiguous to the Eurasian heartland, including the traditional and traditionally frustrating Russian penetration in the Near and Middle East. In the Europe-centered orbit, Russia has a potentially beneficial role to play in preventing the United States from either arrogance or somnolence. But no readily visible effort at countercontainment is likely to nullify America's global material and military primacy, specifically in the non-European world, in the near future. Any reduction in American sway can result only from acts of self-denial which, fostered by self-doubt, may result in partial or complete self-debasement.

The second function of the United States, that of maintaining imperial order, rather than containing a rival power, bears on two types of disorder. At this point we shall indicate them only briefly. One class of disorders—in evidence in Vietnam—consists of acts controlled by an identifiable political will and intelligence; if unchecked, they give rise to international anarchy. The other class of disorders—displayed in the Congo—consists of actions which are in effect uncontrolled by an accountable agent; if allowed to spread, they give rise to chaos. Controlled disorder is intrinsically manageable, while diffuse disorder may become uncontrollable. The latter represents an even greater source of uneasiness than the first, since it threatens not only local positions but also the general predictability of behavior and calculable responsiveness to counteraction, including counterforce. The first threat is to a specific order; the second to the possibility of any order. The first arouses apprehensions; the latter generates a propensity to panic which can spread to otherwise stable bodies politic.

All order, just or unjust, rests in the last resort, if in different degrees, on force. This force—municipal, imperial, or multilateral community force —is employed in conflict with agents defined as those of disorder. Apart from the communist states and the European powers, there are two available instruments for ordering force in the world today: the armed forces of the United States, in principle available for action anywhere, and the few cohesive and usable national armed forces of the lesser states, in principle available only for internal action or, at best, for multilateral peacekeeping operations which are strategically safeguarded by the United States. Where national military force is sufficient to insure order, the United States can abstain from intervening. Where it is not, as was the case in Vietnam, the United States will either have to fight (as the force behind a preferred order) or permit the substitution of a different order or of disorder. There do not seem to be other alternatives.

If this is true, it is not very significant to say that the insertion of American imperial power has made local insufficiencies still more pronounced. The relevant question is whether the American military and related input did or did not more than compensate for the aggravation. Nor is it pertinent to argue that revolutionary disorders succeed only where conditions are favorable to them, especially if the conditions isolated as determining are said to be governmental competence, popular will and support, traditions of submissiveness or sturdiness, and similar broad and ambiguous notions. So phrased the argument is circular and the judgment can only be retrospective. In most cases, conditions will actually be indeterminate and behavior will be susceptible of being swayed toward one or another outcome by the timely application of force. To argue, finally, that each situation of disorder is particular unto itself, responding to local conditions and resources, is to ignore what can be overemphasized but also unduly discounted: the presence or absence in the total environment of a power which, on the basis of precedents, may be regarded as having set the outer limits to tolerated disorder.

Such power, purposefully applied, can at present only be American power. To commit American power to a general role of upholding order would entail not only specific commitments (which may be tacit), but also specific performances (which must be visible). All three—role, commitment, performance—

sharpen the position of the United States as the target of contrary and countered forces. But the position itself derives originally more from the fact that internationally the United States, like any powerful or wealthy group in an unstable and turbulent community, is the inescapable target of all those who are uninterested in legitimacy and express themselves in revolts against the existing order. It is, therefore, unrealistic to try to differentiate specific American interests, in separation from America's position, as the basis for policy; just as it is unrealistic to speculate about America's relation to violent change and revolution as the determinant of wider support for American policy. The position is largely given; the role derives from it with implacable logic; it may only be carried out with variable skill and achieve a variable degree of acceptance as preferable to available alternatives.

To say that an imperial order centered on the United States is presently desirable is not to assert that it is necessarily feasible. Whether it is or not will depend on the ability of the imperial power to manage recurrent conflicts in ways that insure the requisite support at home and efficacy abroad (the necessary, if not sufficient, condition of toleration).

The foremost requirement is the capacity of the imperial nation to manage conflicts with an economy of force. Such economy will often but not always mean deliberately limited force, applied in a routinized and professional manner, scaled to fit local conditions and designed to minimize traumatic strains for the imperial body politic. Events in both the Congo and Vietnam would seem to have demonstrated one thing: there is little room in situations of local disorder for strategies devised for nuclear confrontations between superpowers. It is unwise, in other words, to expect much if anything from, say, deterrence by extant but unused capability, graduated response to unfolding or not reliably identified challenge, or tacit bargaining with the aid of clearly available but conditionally withheld means of punishment. In non-nuclear contests with adversaries in a different order of power and mentality deterrence will often depend on action, not on capability; and economy of force must be observed in conjunction with economy of time, so as not to allow opposition to organize and spread. One may have to buy time by diplomatic or other maneuvers if the capability to act is not yet assembled. If and when such capability is available, however, it will rarely be wise to make a gratuitous gift of time to the other side, even for apparently compelling reasons.

We can only speculate about what could have been achieved in Vietnam by prompt application of American power at the outset of each of the two or three main phases of the conflict—power scaled to fit the real resources of the adversary in the field in South Vietnam and at the controlling centers, rather than scaled to fit the presumed diplomatic and political complexities of the case. An earlier and undisguised action against initial Vietcong operations in particular would at least have unmistakably evidenced American commitment to fight before the adversary convinced himself of his ability to win. In the wake of Vietnam, a ready capability for instant action as well as for "protracted" warfare may become even more important. A new and greater capacity to intervene at tolerable cost may be the only credible evidence of continued American disposition to intervene at all, in any circumstances.

On a par with the capacity to fight limited conflicts is the willingness to intervene frequently—more frequently than Korea and Vietnam. It is not always possible to count on a new generation's forgetting the "never again" of the preceding one. The most common future disorders are likely to be less centrally organized and determinedly aided than in Vietnam; they will also probably be less tenaciously and fanatically backed by force. The communist great powers are apt to be involved in future disorders and conflicts in Asia, Africa, or Latin America. But they are likely to be involved ever less as a matter of revolutionary creed, conscience, or ideological rivalry, and ever more as a matter of great power status and world power ambition. This estimate depends to some extent on a positive conclusion of the ongoing war, at least as far as the American role in the management of such disorders is concerned. It is, however, supported not only by observation of the present but also by contemplation of the past. Presently, one can see on the horizon few actual or potential concentrations of driving energy comparable to the Hanoi-NLF coalition. Historically, for both Rome and Britain, internally ravaging and externally taxing wars tended to mark either the beginning or the decline of imperial power. The going tends to be easier in the middle period of a power's ascendancy. Hence the double-edged prognosis: whatever success the United States achieves in Vietnam will not guarantee a surcease for a pre-eminent America, but will be of compounded value in other places in the future.

A society may, of course, prove weaker than its material power. The United States may abdicate the imperial role in the face of initial frustrations, vindicating one and gambling on the other part of another prognosis: the war in Vietnam—or any other future similar war—cannot be won; but military defeat, clothed in political compromise, would not fatally injure confidence in American arms and resolve, since the revealed weakness would not be seen as that of the imperial power but that of the protected government and people. Barring such abdication, the learning process underway in the American imperial establishment, both military and (one hopes) political, would be of some help should the "never again" become a "once more." The prospect would be still brighter if the learning is paralleled by immunization of the public against excesses in either expectation or dejection during an unwanted type of war.

For the future to remain open, the United States must act on the basis of two convictions. The first conviction affects morale. It holds that a semiconventional, "dirty" war like that in Vietnam is, on balance, preferable to one that is more distasteful and harder to master: wholly diffuse and decentralized force, on the one hand, and wholly concentrated, nuclear force, on the other. The second conviction concerns the sufficiency of American material power for the imperial role. There may have been recently a tendency to exaggerate this power, however superior it is to any other in existence. But, if one has to choose between the illusion of omnipotence and that of impotence, the second is more dangerous than the first. Collision with obstacles will either actualize potential power or regulate the illusion of power. The illusion of insufficient power, by contrast, feeds upon itself by avoiding the test of action.

Public resources can be extended by judicious use, which may generate new, unsuspected resources. Substantial costs of the imperial role in, say, inflation and short-term deflection of resources and skills from civilian pursuits may be unavoidable, though this is not certain, but there are also potential gains, such as the generation of a new sense of purpose and of enlarged opportunities where before there were group divisions and an individual sense of drift. Moreover, properly adjusted public finance ought to be able to supply the means for professionalizing the American military and political establishments in their imperial role. There are, again, political and moral costs in thus insulating the larger body politic from all but very large-scale foreign involvements. But the advantages are greater and the costs can be kept in bounds by the very size of the civic interest and civilian power in the United States. Professionalism would permit the majority to go on generating assets without major upheaval, and it would contribute to the social rehabilitation and vocational qualification of the participating under-privileged members of society.

Expansion of military professionalism is liable to be opposed as the opening wedge of professional militarism and civic apathy. But it ought to be noted in this connection that a like approach to economic and political development has received widening support in regard to much weaker, undeveloped communities over the years. It may be the only answer to the problem of order now that distaste for war in industrial societies has outpaced any waning of its causes or decline in its incidence in the rest of the world.

There are two main grounds on which to object to the preceding analysis. One line of argument accepts conflict and disorder as endemic, but holds that local disorders will take care of themselves, if left alone, and that competent local defenders of established order will save themselves, if not compromised or overwhelmed by outside power. This line of argument stresses the most common state of affairs to the detriment of the exceptional and thus critical cases. The other line of argument rejects the normal in favor of the exceptional. It finds the idea of recurrent conflict intolerable and seeks refuge in visions of futuristic possibilities in international relations. In this view, the application of traditional precepts to international politics is wrong because these ideas hinder or prevent the evolution of a better order. The principal identified enemy of the new world of interdependence, integration, development, and pacific conflict-resolution will vary. Once it was the cold war and the Soviet or the American ruling classes committed to it; now it is American bellicosity and interference. The key factors propelling international society toward a placid new world are alternately held to be the self-neutralizing excess of nuclear power in the hands of the strong; the absence of power and the commitment to power-free interstate relations of the weak; and the onward progress of industrialization. For those who believe in these forces, American action ought to be at once ample and amicable, working simultaneously through vast amounts of economic aid, to create new goods, and through nimble diplomacy, to prevent old disputes from turning into new crises.

Such prescriptions are superficially appealing. The advocates of reform can, however, misrepresent its possibilities, just as advocates of revolution misrepresent the benefits of violent upheavals. They would be almost as irresponsible if they applied their theories literally to the conduct of national policy. It is not politically responsible to ask statesmen to initiate, in relations with underdeveloped states, changes which are far from common or possible even within the most advanced countries—for example, redistributing wealth without retaining control over the process, or resolving group conflicts while they are yet dormant. And it is intellectually shallow to stress the material interdependence of nations as a sufficient basis for unequivocal policy conclusions at a time when states can increasingly choose with whom and how to be interdependent. France today is interdependent with the United States and the NATO allies in respect to economics and even somewhat to military strategy. In diplomatic strategy, however, France is interdependent with the Soviet Union and its allies. Such contradictions render the exercise of an imperial role more difficult; they are not, however, to be taken as merely obscuring underlying harmonies that make it redundant.

Any prescription for policy is as correct or as mistaken as the underlying analysis of the nature of politics. The contemporary international system comprises varied strands of relations. It comprises the relatively new kind of political relations between industrial states with fading or temporarily overshadowed conflicts—in the western European and Atlantic area. It comprises the half-new, half-traditional kind of relations between the nuclear superpowers who share the power to destroy and the interest to retain near-monopoly. The principal new element in these relations is increased caution and avoidance of force. The system also comprises an almost wholly traditional or orthodox strand, which is usually found in the crudely realistic relations between underdeveloped states in contest over local assets or regional leadership; and between the established world powers and the non-nuclear or weak nuclear powers that seek regional dominance. The relatively active, major and middle powers—notably the United States, Soviet Union, China, and France—are both linked and divided by conflicts of widely differing intensity, enacted through means with widely different components of military power. They are second-guessed even more than seconded by relatively passive background powers such as India, Japan, and Great Britain. With the exception of China, they like to behave in an orthodox and even classic manner with one another and pretend to be revolutionary (or prorevolution) when they address themselves to the less-developed states.

No one kind of international politics or relations is or can be all-encompassing, but one of the strands will set the tone and be controlling in the last resort. One determinant is the identity of the dominant conflict of the day. Whether still residing in the American-Soviet contest for global preponderance or already shifting to an American-Chinese contest over primacy in the third world, the dominant conflict of today is certainly at bottom an orthodox power-political contest, however circumscribed it may be by the nuclear setting and its revolutionary frame of reference. As long as alignment and other policies continue to respond to tangible and immediate preoccupations, the development issue along the North-South axis will remain of secondary importance in its capacity to sway diplomacy. The other, and perhaps crucial, determinant of the kind of politics which sets the tone for the international system will be the distinctive assets and comparative advantage of the leading nation, whenever there is such a nation. The United States is such a nation today. The distinctive American power assets are undoubtedly conventional rather than revolutionary, if we take the twentieth rather than the eighteenth century for our yardstick, and conventional rather than nuclear, if we adopt the yardstick of use and efficacy.

Our era is, on balance, revolutionary in tone and imbued with continuities in every other respect. New or updated modes and practices are not without bearing on the exercise of any, and least of all imperial, power. They constitute new restraints and comprise new instruments and opportunities; they inhibit action and supply new rationalizations for both action and the avoidance of action. But the elements of the new politics make the exercise of imperial power neither odious nor obsolete. In the absence of a major reversal of existing trends, it will take a very long time at best for traditional politics to be more than marginally modified by the methods peculiar to the development politics between South and North, to industrial politics within western Europe and between it and North America, or to the dimension of pure nuclear politics between the superpowers. The first two are, in traditional terms, the politics of adaptation to little or unequal power; all three are, with some differences, the politics of unusable or hard-to-use military power, and all, especially the last, are only imperfectly practiced and understood. They are really no more than variations on traditional means and ends, with an admixture of simulation in regard to both.

A real change in international relations, which would bring with it a fundamental modification of America's solitary imperial role, would probably result only from the dissemination of nuclear weapons among less-developed and potentially less-responsible states. If such nuclear capabilities were primitive and, therefore, destabilizing by inviting a first strike, the two superpowers would be pushed toward joint responsibility in order to control a more explosive environment. Such control might be merely the partially unintended result of an adversary posture. This would occur if each superpower were to substitute its own nuclear capability for the primitive capabilities of its protégé in a local confrontation, so as to elevate the deterrent relationship to the more stable superpower level and thus gain time for settlements by conventional political or military means. Or control might become self-consciously cooperative, rather than the result of adversary positions. It might lead to joint confiscation or destruction of the nuclear capabilities of the "irresponsible" states. This would concretize the so-called negative community of interests between the superpowers over nuclear weaponry into a positive condominium in regard to political upheavals. The negative community has thus far been expressed in general treaties or treaty drafts; co-responsibility for the world community would imply quite specific transactions. It would also necessitate, as well as permit, greater American tolerance for Soviet interventions across great distances. The conventional capability for such intervention could be funded out of savings from abatement in the Soviets' nuclear competition with the United States.

New conditions of this kind would have their pitfalls. Most importantly, the superpowers would stand in an uncertain relationship to the larger nuclear powers, which would be less susceptible than really small states to superpower control or to interference with their own local control devices; some of them at least might not be sufficiently restrained by nuclear status to forego exploiting disorders attendant on proliferation. But all this is hypothetical. International politics today is largely a matter of waiting and, for the more vigorous states, keeping ready for developments which may not even occur. It seems more plausible, however, that China instead of achieving the status of a major nuclear power may relapse into chaos than that world order can be built upon frustration of an evolutionary process: that of assimilating nuclear weaponry by allowing it to spread among the qualified, industrial states, and by their adapting to it. This development cannot be stopped; it can only be managed. When nuclear diffusion has run its course, the result will be a changed ranking of powers and, possibly, a changed character of international politics involving a changed role for the United States.

For the time being, however, one reason for keeping American capacity and propensity to intervene intact is that both will be useful in managing dissemination—either by employing intervention to bar nuclear acquisition where it would be clearly premature in terms of economic and political maturity or by conspicuously withholding intervention to accelerate progress toward nuclear and other self-sufficiency in the interest of regional stability. Other things being equal, retrenchment in American "globalism" can come only when multilateral deterrence among the nuclear powers is combined with effective controls over the acquisition and use of nuclear weapons by countries with an insufficient stake in peace and order. At that time in the future, American retrenchment will come automatically. It will be not only possible but also necessary, not only spontaneous but largely enforced. The reason is evident. The nuclearized parties to regional multilateral deterrence relationships will be reluctant to invest the United States with anything more than a discreet background role. By its mere existence a global nuclear power would then discourage resort to nuclear strikes by any one regional state, since the latter would have to attack the global power pre-emptively or face its disapproval from a position further weakened relatively by the regional exchange. Such a background role would go well with sponsorship of regional and global organizations calculated to reflect and restrain the new multi-power nuclear politics.

Hopeful possibilities for the future of world politics have come to depend, to a yet undefinable extent, on a positive outcome of the Vietnam conflict. This is especially true for relations among the great powers, and between the two superpowers in particular. There are three aspects to this: the character of the war in Vietnam as a substitute for World War III, the effect of the war in Vietnam on the relationship between conventional and nuclear force, and the war's effect on the relationship between controlled and uncontrolled local violence.

The first aspect can be conveyed by the following

assertion. In conditions making a total war among great powers unpalatable, military substitutes become necessary to reinforce the impact of typically inconclusive nonmilitary substitutes for war. One such substitute is a direct confrontation of the Cuban type. Another is a local engagement in which one or both of the superpowers participate. Such an engagement, if sufficiently serious, will unavoidably develop into a test of will and resolve of the major states, whether they participate directly or not. It represents a vital clarification of the powers' usable strength in relation to one another. The adversary relationship between the United States and the Soviet Union has been increasingly qualified by latent elements of consensus; the adversary relationship between the United States and Communist China has been at once more strident and less specific. Against this background, the war in Vietnam tests the will and capability of these powers with results which will either confirm the presently suspected outcome of the cold war (as essentially favorable to the United States) or reopen the issue of the outcome. The shooting war, which is America's first imperial war, is also a contention carried over from the Stalinist era. It may well appear in retrospect as the last and culminating engagement in the cold war, imposed on two reluctant superpowers by forward or failing allies and protégés.

The cold war can be seen, in a politico-strategic sense, as a functional equivalent of World War III. As a war-substitute, it was waged by means of the sublimated devices of the arms race, competition over economic growth, political propaganda, and the contest over decolonization. It was punctuated by overt clashes over Berlin, Korea, and Cuba in particular. Before Vietnam, however, this world-war substitute lacked a major and specific military catalyst which would bring into the open the terminal relationship of forces between the two super-powers and compel its acceptance. Such demonstration and acceptance are not displays of strength and sobriety for their own sakes. They have a highly creative potential, notably if they remain implicit, at a time when the hitherto dominant political conflict undergoes basic changes favorable to long-term adjustments between the principal cold war rivals. These demonstrations indicate what the stronger party can, and the weaker must, concede to the other.

In this respect, the war in Vietnam has complemented the confrontation over Cuba. The missile crisis established United States global mastery on the strategic-nuclear level for as long as this country is willing to maintain it. It also confirmed America's naval paramountcy. Vietnam can either consummate or largely nullify the cold war and Cuban accomplishments—depending on whether it establishes America's superior capacity for effectively intervening in a distant and uncongenial military theater.

The second long-term aspect of the war in Vietnam has to do with conventional and nuclear weapons. It is in the American and the general interest to secure growing Soviet cooperation in the maintenance of order in an increasingly nuclear environment. The United States is more likely to secure such cooperation if it retains its over-all primacy. Primacy does not rule out occasional failings which in turn permit the Soviet Union to enhance its status by issuing a challenge or rendering a service to the embarrassed hegemon; but it is incompatible with a major retreat. In the environment of nuclear proliferation, it would be more than ever important that conventional and nuclear capabilities retain their present division of labor. In this division, conventional force is employed to permit positive action, while nuclear power is used to deter intolerable action by other states and may be used to stimulate concerted action by major nuclear powers. Such concerted action can best be rendered both mandatory and decisive if there is only occasional, abusive resort to nuclear force by secondary states; it would be rendered difficult or impossible by a widespread resort to such force, affecting or infecting the superpowers themselves.

It is in this light that one ought to view the likely consequences of an American failure in Vietnam. It would be apt to reverse the present trend toward international relations which are conventional, non-nuclear, and nonrevolutionary, especially for the dominating relationships involving at least one superpower. This trend has been characterized by three main features. The first two are the progressive assimilation of nuclear force as a mere background factor and ultimate restraint and the gradual de-ideologization of the foreign relations of the communist states. Both of these trends are being confirmed by China's hysteric reactions against them. The superpowers themselves confirm the trend when they stress a hypothetical nuclear problem—proliferation—as the "real" military danger to world security, and when they look to this problem for the possibility of a traditional great power concert between them which would offset the residually revolutionary contest in and over Vietnam. The third aspect of the trend toward orthodoxy has been the tentatively restored primacy of conventional weapons and strategy. Naval power resolved the missile threat in Cuba; conventional military power made it possible in Vietnam to come to grips with an enemy who could not be matched on the plane of his preferred guerrilla force and strategy.

The trend toward conventional international politics, if sustained, is the best safeguard for an explosive world; it ought to be protected and reinforced by all disposable means. Should conventional military power suffer defeat in Vietnam, international politics might very well come to polarize around the two remaining, and thus presumably the only efficacious, means of force: nuclear weapons and insidious terror. It would not be surprising if such polarization were eventually matched by increasing antagonism between the supporters of the status quo and those who oppose it. The increasingly civilized contest between the United States and the Soviet Union, and the somewhat less civilized controversy between the hawks and the doves in this country, would then appear in retrospect as but a highly publicized but ephemeral reasoning together.

III. ELEMENTARY ORDER AND PRE-EMINENT POWER

In the contemporary international arena, elementary order is *not* a complete absence of the use of force. Consequently, to uphold elementary order is not to set out to prevent use of force regardless of whether it is defensive or offensive and, when offensive, whether employed to thwart or punish a threat or to achieve aggrandizement. To eliminate all force would amount, at best, to a maximum or perfect order; at worst, and not uncommonly, to supreme injustice, in the absence of alternative means for change and redress.

A moderate definition of order does not over-commit the policing power and does not rule out certain kinds of turbulence that have a beneficial political potential. Thus external use of force may promote both the political development of less-developed countries and the creation of an autochthonous balance of power in a region. It does so by providing a test of viability, and it can supply needed evidence that even unstable or insecure governments are ready to uphold the state's interest. Being a test of the regime's realism in assessing its capability, the use of force also tests the people's operative idealism, which alone can convert capability into power. Internationally tolerable conflicts include military engagements between India and Pakistan, Morocco and Algeria, and, with qualifications, Israel and the Arab states. Conflicts are tolerable when outside power and pressure can at any stage impose either a rough parity of force between contestants or self-restraint on the victor. In such conflicts, after failing to prevent local wars, the United States may well confine itself to merely hindering exacerbation from the outside. The main objective here is to safeguard American capacity for exerting influence in the ensuing diplomatic contest over political settlement, rather than a quick termination of the conflict on any terms.

Recourse to arms can frequently facilitate a settlement. This is true especially between relatively new and less-developed states, when such recourse is needed to satisfy the honor of one or both contestants or to establish their relative strength. Satisfaction of individual honor and determination of relative power may even take the place of substantive settlement, either temporarily or permanently. This was largely the case for Morocco and Pakistan and might have been so for the Arabs, if the fighting had gone more favorably for them. A very lopsided contest, however, clearly favoring one party, is unlikely to facilitate or replace settlement, unless the disparity is so great as to eliminate the inferior party as an independent actor. Any newly contrived distribution may be hard to assimilate in an acceptable structure of rights and power in the area. One can only speculate when the gains and losses would be assimilable and when not. It would have been one thing for Morocco, or for Morocco and Mali jointly, to absorb a Mauritania apparently unable to develop an independent identity, while the annexing state or states were satisfying intrinsically limited ethnic or historic claims. Such absorption would have been a change justifiable in terms of order and easy to assimilate by the regional system, especially in conjunction with the simultaneous rise to independence of a strong Algeria. It would be quite another thing, and the implications for order would be more explosive, were Algeria to absorb Tunisia, or Israel absorb Jordan, in what could legitimately be regarded as the beginning of an ongoing process of regional expansion and domination.

Social and communal perturbations in the domestic order, too, need not give rise to international concern with order. They may be, and often are, the necessary incidents in defining a community capable of inner cohesion, development, or both. Political and economic development will not follow a straight line forward, but will rather amount to a haphazard process of learning and adjustment. Even if a perturbation appears to be inspired by communist actors or associated with them, it should satisfy in most cases the interest in elementary order to rope off the area, especially one that is not adjacent to a powerful communist state. The hope is then that the local communists and their allies will prove unable to create any greater perturbation than can a man caught in quicksand.

Favorable developments of this kind took place in the 1950s and 1960s in Syria and Iraq, in Zanzibar off the coast of Africa, and in former French Guinea in Africa. All these countries were relatively remote from a major communist power. In Guinea, the process was aided by the determined, and widely criticized, action of France, which pushed Guinea into an exclusive, educational contact with the communist powers. In the case of Syria and in Zanzibar, internal opposition was strong enough to defeat the internal threat in an association with a more stable country—Egypt and Tanganyika, respectively. The conclusion emerges that in instances where action remains possible, even if it is not instantaneous, the United States should wait out the first major reaction to radicalism. If the reaction tends to counteract the upheaval, things are likely to settle down without American intervention. However, should the disturbance prove to be cumulative and spread by way of imitation, export, or both, as appeared to be the case and still may prove to be the case with Castroism in Latin America, there will be a strong case for intervention, if only to demonstrate the will to stop a possible chain reaction.

By contrast, elementary order is at stake if violence or other coercive pressure is exerted in ways and for ends tantamount to international anarchy or chaos. International anarchy must not be equated with war. Rather, it entails an erosion or debasement of the standards of international behavior and interstate conflict. It is generated by deliberate and controlled employment of force or other coercive pressure which is locally disproportionate in magnitude, unmanageable or demoralizing in mode, and indeterminate in thrust. If left unchecked, such use of force can escalate to the point where it would be too costly for any ordering influence, individual or collective, to master.

The criteria of anarchy concern both goals and means. If the goals are expansive or indeterminate, they will require the backing of major force if they are to have a chance to succeed. The resulting local or regional imperialism, when unchecked or apparently irresistible, is the principal source of international anarchy. With regard to means, anarchy threatens when the mode of relevant behavior and the kind of force or coercion employed are difficult or impossible to oppose without resort to equivalent measures—such as infiltration, subversion, assassination of leaders, terrorization or deportation of politically passive populations.

The magnitude and the methods of locally employed power are, it would seem, the decisive criteria from the perspective of world order. It is, consequently, not a decisive consideration for the United States whether the local or regional imperialism is communist or noncommunist: it can be engaged in by Sukarno's Indonesia, by Ho Chi Minh's Vietnam, by Communist China, or by Gandhian India. Expansion can be pursued, by Egypt in the name of Pan-Arabism or Arab socialism and by Israel in the name of Zionism or Israeli security, by Cuba on behalf of Castroism, or by a future Argentina on behalf of an updated variety of Peronism. There is, however, one aspect of expansion which is especially relevant for the United States as the power with the greatest stake in the existing degree of world order. This is the ultimate thrust of such expansionism, whatever its averred goal. The key concern is whether the drive to overthrow the existing distribution of power, authority, and rights, or to preclude its natural evolution, also aims at obstructing U.S. access to the area by means short of massive force.

The regime in North Vietnam qualified for American opposition by these standards. Independently or in collusion with Communist China it set out to destroy, first by sponsorship of subversion and later directly, any future chance for a balance of relatively autonomous power among the lesser states of former Indochina and, by plausible extension, of Southeast Asia. The related goal was to bar American access and participation in the shaping of such a balance or balances. It is because Sukarno had a similar and apparently self-perpetuating ambition, first against West New Guinea and then against Malaysia, that he too ought to have been overtly "confronted" by the United States rather than deviously countered by way of support for internal and British opposition.

American action against noncommunist expansionism is also mandatory because it alone can demonstrate ideological impartiality and, therefore, the credibility of the larger American purpose and of its predictability in implementation. For these reasons—the acceptance and thus legitimacy for its imperial role—the United States will have to curb Israel's present ambitions and some of its practices in the Near East, should they continue unabated.

International order also has a domestic dimension, in that tribal, class, regional, or communal strife can easily become unpredictable in the magnitude, mode, and ultimate thrust of violence. To differentiate this type of disorder from international anarchy, we call it here, in its extreme form, chaos. World order is at stake when this type of turbulence does not remain confined and isolated, but instead ramifies abroad, either by the design and doing of other states or by its own internal dynamic. Involvement of extraneous powers in internal disorders can in turn vary in intensity. It has been greater in the 1960s in the Belgian Congo and Yemen than in Nigeria or Colombia, for instance. When, by contrast, internal disorders spread to other countries or generate a pervasive atmosphere conducive to violence by their own momentum, external ramification is less immediately explosive but may be more difficult for international or extraneous agents to cope with. Although international involvement in the Congo was on the whole contained, propensity to violence spread to other African countries, most prominently to Nigeria, on a scale which has justified international concern even if it did not warrant any but indirect counteraction. Actual or potential breakup in and of new countries that often perpetuate accidental colonial boundaries—for example, the Congo, Nigeria, Indonesia—ought to be judged individually. Significant criteria are the prospective viability of the dissident group in terms of its size and the intensity of its opposition to the central authority—an intensity which is apt to reflect the strength of the group and of its grievances.

The two types of disorder—chaos and anarchy —converge when a grossly inadequate economic performance leads to attempts to compensate externally for internal stagnation and instability. Nkrumah's Ghana and Sukarno's Indonesia fall into this category. By contrast, other unstable and inadequately developing countries like Burma and India have been satisfied with reflecting their internal conditions in foreign policies that are no more than wayward. They are almost as difficult to fit into a coherent structure of world order.

Unchecked international ramifications of internal decay and turbulence affect the United States and its role in the maintenance of order in several ways. They tend, first, to inhibit American access to the area because they give rise to anti-Americanism. Second, they are likely to compel the United States to share whatever access it retains. Third, internal breakdown of public order in one country can set off cumulative international chaos in areas where order is always precarious. Somewhat like international anarchy, such chaos is not to be equated with just any violence. It stands rather for a chain reaction of uncontrollable violence which makes conventional ordering power inadequate once the turbulence has been allowed to exceed a certain intensity or scope. The Congo is in this category—a fact which was responsible for two American unilateral interventions in that country after the U.N.'s withdrawal.

If acted upon with some consistency and a judicious mix of instruments, these broad criteria of elementary order and action against disorder do not cast the United States in the role of an omnipresent policeman. For the United States the criteria imply no more (if no less) than continuous readiness for policing action wherever it is necessary to keep the flow of international life moving in the general direction of an authentic, multiregional system. The goal is a self-sustaining global system rather than one sustained by the power of a single state or by the ramifying conflict of the two most powerful states. To this end, in the vital, formative period of the system some entity must preserve the basic conditions for individual or collective self-help by those organized groups (states, factions, or parties) threatened by international anarchy or chaos. Once one admits the need for such an ordering function, it becomes a matter of expediency whether a policing action is carried out by the leading world power in cooperation with other powers and the United Nations, whenever possible and sufficient, or unilaterally, whenever necessary as an alternative to collective failure.

The above concepts of order and order maintenance could be challenged on several grounds. They seemingly overburden the United States in the interest of essentially procedural desiderata stressing, first, a mode or style of behavior and, second, access to local situations; and they do so without explicitly establishing the relationship of the procedural desiderata either to present American national interests or to an envisaged global structure and distribution of power. All these factors are interrelated, although style is more closely related to structure, and access to the capacity to undertake international tasks. The problem of "national interest" stands alone and will be taken up first.

National interest so broadly conceived as to coincide with the maintenance of order may best be called "imperial interest." Imperial interest is not to be confused with supranational interest. The latter is related to a new entity superseding the nation-state, while the former aims at developing a coherent policy for a pre-eminent nation-state among other nation-states. Imperial interest is neither the sum of specific national interests nor of group interests. But just as supranational or group considerations might militate against the national interest, calculation from specific national interests might undermine the imperial interest of a power which has outgrown the conventional format of a nation-state without assuming any clearly distinguishable new character. To illustrate: The United States has certain specific interests in the Middle East. As a maritime nation, its interest is to keep open the passage for American and other vessels in the Suez Canal. As an alliance leader, the United States is interested in maintaining the flow of oil from the Middle East to western Europe. As one of two principal contenders on the plane of a continuing, if uneven, bipolarity, it has an interest in checking or at least controlling Soviet political and naval penetration into the Eastern Mediterranean. As a delicately balanced pluralistic political system and as a society committed to certain humanitarian values, the United States has an interest in the continuance of the state of Israel as an independent entity. There may be other such specifically "national" interests. Some of them are complementary; others are or occasionally appear to be mutually exclusive. American policy in regard to the Middle East is apt to vacillate unless it superimposes upon the shifting balance of such national interests a set of principles derived from America's concerns in other parts of the world. These concerns can be subsumed under the notion of "world order," even if only as a condition of national security or integrity. The conditions of effective global action over time can then be subsumed under the notion of imperial interest, if only to identify formally the broader considerations adjudicating between specific national interests when these are in conflict.

This is not to deny that specific, national interests can be differentiated in the degree of their importance and direct bearing on security. Yet, except in the few and exceptional crisis situations when national security is manifestly at stake, appeal to specific interests will help discipline the discussion of policy rather than determine its content. Too much stress on specific interests will tend to produce inaction, in the name of prudence, or incoherent action, in the name of compromise. And even if those responsible for the foreign policy of an imperial state do not mistake the breadth of interests for their undifferentiable equivalence, they still will be led to assess interests differently in the imperial context than they would in a strictly national one. They will do so not least because of their awareness of the demonstration effect of action in one set of circumstances for actors in another, comparable set of circumstances and of the tendency of others, friends and foes alike, to impute to the imperial state as interest that which for a lesser country can at best be an ideal or a desideratum. Attribution of this kind will tend to be sufficiently significant for policy to impart to such imputed interests much of the weight of intrinsic interests—interests, that is, pertaining to the conditions of national security strictly conceived.

Such imputed interests will progressively affect the conception of imperial interests, as a body of interests encompassing national security and international order, security and status, the substance and symbols of power, domestic and international stability. The practical scope of the imperial interest will in most situations be determined by national capability or power rather than by imperatives of immediate national security. The difficulty to have the body politic as a whole consistently perceive the broadly interpreted imperial interest as a valid basis for taxing action will, moreover, increase the importance of organizing national power so as to make it usable even in periods of fluctuating or failing national will—not least in order to avoid the necessity for overstating an issue of international order as one of national security. The intellectual indolence and political opportunism underlying the habit of formulating all demanding policy in terms of vital interests affecting national security are self-defeating for any state with more than sporadic external involvement. The reflex, once acquired, will sooner or later discredit the policy and the policy-makers alike. It will give rise to an often vain quest for a palpable archenemy and to affirmations of contingent vulnerability inapplicable to a nation at once supremely secure in terms of conventional military power and unavoidably (if very hypothetically) insecure in terms of ultimate nuclear power.

How the United States goes about defining and implementing this imperial interest will depend on the preferred kind of world order it adopts in the different areas, The United States could, for instance, promote regional balances of power between local powers, or it could delegate order-maintaining functions to particularly close regional allies. The choice ought to be influenced by a multiregional perspective—that is, a judgment of what is desirable and feasible for most or all of the regions to which the United States has access. In the absence of such perspective, actual choices will be no more than unwitting and ever-shifting adaptations to current events in any one region. Once adopted, however, the preference will determine how to weight conflicting U.S. national interests in relation to all regions. Using the Middle East as an example, one kind of globally determined bias might translate into a regional policy which strengthens Israel to the point of nearly irreversible superiority over the Arabs; another bias would aim at redressing the balance in favor of the Arabs.

In clarifying the meaning of the imperial interest, we have moved into the problem of the structure of power and order. Structure—bearing here specifically on regional balances or paramountcies—may be usefully discussed in connection with the problem of the mode or style of action, such as subversion or expansionism. The greater the ambiguity in promoting a particular configuration of power as a basis of order, the less naive or formalistic will it be to stress modes of behavior as the stuff of order. Regarding structure, an academic distinction between international "order" and "system" has great practical implication. Order is a pattern of relations which are tolerable in terms of particular values and general stability in the short run. A system is a pattern of interactions which are broadly predictable in terms of particular interests and susceptible of recovering stability after a period of upheaval. If order is to be maintained, any upsetting behavior or change must be contained close to its source; the system requires merely that any such disturbance be eventually assimilated. While order can and has to be managed, the system maintains itself and evolves as the unintended result of individual actions. Consequently, the crucial features of an international system have to do with the identity of states and their ranking and configuration; behavior is presumed to follow. Conversely, order is a function of the kind of behavior which will tend to safeguard states and their established rights against abrupt and forcible changes in the structures of power and interest. Thus, major conventional war or nuclear proliferation may be regarded as contrary to international order in the short run. By contrast, a particular major war may be necessary to re-balance the international system, or nuclear proliferation may be deemed indispensable for the reconstitution of an authentically global international system.

Enough has been said to indicate a paradox: to work for any kind of world order is likely to impede somewhat the crystallization of an international system of states. An international system depends on the formation and reformation of state-actors with well-understood interests, on the clarification of power relationships, and on the routinization of diplomatic relationships among viable states. All this has occurred in the past, and can occur in the future, through conflict of all kinds. The evolution of a European or any other international system is the story of conflicts which create the system and then later on lead to its destruction. This phenomenon has to be admitted before it can be usefully fitted into a workable scheme of order in theory or practice. But, more generally, the contradiction between the conditions of managed order and those of an evolving system remains, especially in regard to tolerable kinds, magnitudes, and thrusts of force. Because of this contradiction, the mode of action rather than the structure of power is the more proper criterion of even a pragmatic policy committed to the maintenance of order.

There is a practical reason for stressing tolerable modes of behavior on a par with or above desirable structures or configurations of power. While it is possible to identify immediately disturbing behavior, it is difficult or impossible to anticipate the implications of structural trends. The issue is highlighted by the problem of regional imperialism. We have already noted that the United States can in principle favor two patterns of multiregional world order. One consists of regional balances of power, encompassing and up to a point shielding the very small states, with different degrees and forms of organization to match and mute power differentials. The other pattern is that of regionally dominant powers, organizing and policing an area with or without either the disguises of multilateral organization or the restraints of an expanded balance-of-power system (comprised of such aggrandized regional states plus the world power or powers). In principle, China, Japan, India, Indonesia, and Australia could make up such a balance of power, thus supplanting the different Asian and Pacific subregions as separate areas of competition. Likewise, the inadequate balancing of power in the Middle East and adjoining areas could evolve into an Afro-Asian balance comprising powers which have emerged aggrandized from preliminary competitions in the Middle East, sub-Saharan Africa, South and North Africa, and the Persian Gulf area. While each of the subregional core-powers would be surrounded by weak or client states, the role of the world power or powers would be hard to predict; it could be either more or less difficult to implement actively than in the smaller theaters.

Either structural alternative—regional balance or paramountcy—has something to be said for it from the viewpoint of world order and system as well as of American interests. In terms of world order, different costs are likely to be incurred while achieving one or the other pattern and in maintaining it; only the cost of achieving the pattern of regional paramountcies is relatively certain and apt to be high in terms of pre-existing rights. In terms of the international system, the issue is neutral, with an edge for regional paramountcies in the less-developed areas, insofar as they are more likely to produce well-defined actors with predictable relations among themselves. Such a pattern would fit nicely into a unifocal international system.[1] It would facilitate the tasks of the globally dominant state as long as the regionally dominant states were willing to act in unison with it. The present debate over the scope of American involvements revolves around this question while often sidestepping its implications. The countries singled out as worthy of U.S. intervention if threatened, such as Japan, India, and Israel, are eminently eligible for the role of regional great-power lieutenants of the United States. The question is how much and how long these or other such countries would act in accord with American aims. They would probably have to differentiate their policies from those of the United States in order to achieve a position of regional leadership with local support or consent: they would almost certainly come into conflict with the United States if attempts to uphold regional order are perceived by the U.S. as local domination.

A reluctant Japan has become the western favorite for relieving a downgraded India in the role of major regional power. A more willing candidate for regional leadership in her part of Asia has been Indonesia—unilaterally assertive under Sukarno and more discreet and multilaterally oriented under his successors. Israel has seemed to waver between pursuing regional balance and preponderance in ways reflecting the vicissitudes of internal struggle for leadership, military fortunes, and American support. A speedy rise to regional paramountcy of any of these states would infringe upon many established

---

[1] On the "unifocal international system" see my *Imperial America: The International Politics of Primacy* (Baltimore: The John Hopkins Press, 1967), pp. 36ff.

positions and interests; a slow, dragging progression toward regional leadership would entail a protracted and widening conflict. The imperial interest of the United States in world order might well suffer more from such developments than its national interest could profit as a result of partial disengagement.

Regarding Israel, there is much to be said for close cooperation with an Israel organically attached to the American body politic and expanding its role in an area of shifting, unstable, and easily antagonized forces. Yet the American imperial interest would be compromised by identification with an Israeli policy of expansion, which would reduce the Arab population in occupied or adjoining areas to an inferior status and place Israel in a position comparable to that of South Africa in regard to black Africans. The United States may eventually fall back on alliances with strong points like South Africa and Israel if the third world becomes hopelessly fluid or hostile. But it is unlikely that the United States could indefinitely apply a double standard: one policy against South Africa and another for Israel.

In the case of Indonesia, the imperial and the national interests could be likewise at variance. The United States might have countenanced Sukarno's foreign policy on the assumption that an expansive Indonesia would eventually come into conflict with an expansive China, even if, or especially if, the two expansionists were initially allied. Such a conflict would lead an augmented but chastened Indonesia back to the United States; it would have resulted in the creation of a strong state in the area, a worthwhile recipient of American development assistance.

But uncertainties arise at this point. Once ascendant, Indonesia might seek to escape alignment with any of the world powers and establish an autarchic regional system or make common cause with a like-minded regional power, such as Japan. In the end, the United States, or any world or multiregional power, might have to cope with a much greater problem than that of managing weak states and promoting some balance of power among them. The price of neatness may be too high.

These uncertainties do not rule out the necessity for deciding which power structure to favor. But they do increase the short-term significance of modes of behavior and related aspects when deciding which conditions of action to promote or discourage in the interest of order. In the case of regional expansionism, the means with which expansion is promoted can be more or less incompatible with order. This aspect is important in itself. But it is even more important in relation to a second aspect: whether the target of the expansionist drive is a viable entity or only an artificial creation that is apt to provoke endless upheavals as long as it exists. A crucial, if not always self-sufficient, test of viability is the capacity to resist pressure. Some modes of pressure are, however, less conclusive than others; those which depress the standards of international relations are by and large the least conclusive. It is too simple to argue that the political regime unable to withstand subversion is unfit to survive because it lacks sophistication or popular support. Actually, advanced political civilizations may be most vulnerable to subversion, while majority popular support, even where it exists, may take too long to translate into a winning countersubversion strategy.

Another critical aspect has to do with the likely ultimate scope of an immediately upsetting expansion. One standard is the rationale of expansion, which may or may not be self-limiting. Historical rights or ethnic affinities usually have built-in limits, while ideological stimuli tend to override external limits. Other indicators of scope include whether the expansionist drive is backed by a contiguous major power and whether the critical area has the physical and psychological capacity for resistance. On the basis of such criteria, a strictly limited Israeli expansionism carried out with overt means and without collusion with a major power might be regarded as less at variance with world order than the more ambiguous expansionism of Indonesia under Sukarno. Indonesian expansionism would be, by the same token, less objectionable than that of the North Vietnamese. And Chinese expansionism would be the most objectionable of all, especially if it were in some respects and under certain circumstances backed or shielded by Soviet Russia.

As an imperial power, the United States will be concerned about all such features. In terms of its strictly national interests, the United States should be most concerned about the scope of expansion and whether there is great-power backing, especially if the great power is hostile. It is questionable, however, whether American foreign policy can be wholly controlled by only one range of criteria. If too long-term a view is taken—visualizing an expansionist Indonesia, Japan, or North Vietnam of the future offsetting a stronger China—then there are few present threats to world order unequivocal enough to justify costly action. In fact, the difference between international order and system is unknowingly effaced; management is surrendered to evolution and the otherwise intolerable is tolerated as a way station to the predicted, if unpredictable, future. Yet world order is a matter of a precisely envisaged, concrete distribution of power, not of hypothetical distribution in the long run. The United States as an imperial power ought not to be unduly concerned about the hypothetical risks implicit in any reordering of interstate relations— as long as the reordering takes place in an "orderly" fashion. But neither should the United States be unduly impressed by the hypothetical advantages which might accrue from a reordering which, ideally, would convert presently hostile but strengthened states like North Vietnam into friends or at least neutrals without jeopardizing the amity of activated states like Japan.

Finally, the United States must assess which, if any, basic reordering is likely to occur in the near future in a relatively straightforward fashion. The prospects are not bright for the peaceable evolution of regional balance-of-power systems under American auspices in Southeast Asia, the Middle East, or Africa. But chances may be brighter now than in years past as histrionic anticolonialism recedes and as America's imperial role is increasingly accepted by most states as being indispensable. The prospects are further improved if, in the case of most less-developed states, "balances of power" are taken to comprise "pools of impotence," to wit, stalemates and strategies resulting from incapacity to exert organized offensive power in a sustained manner and for an irreversible effect. It is still less likely that the near future will see an orderly advance toward the assumption of either responsibility for regional order or supremacy in regional orders of power by so-called middle powers, coupled with their ready toleration of American supervision. There will have to be much prodding of the reluctant and restraining of the overly eager candidates before America's supervision of regionally decentralized order could supplant her stewardship of the ongoing process which is viewed as possibly culminating in such multiregional order. For the time being, and leaving aside China, the most frequently named candidates for a leading regional role—whether Japan, India, Indonesia, Algeria, Nigeria, or Brazil—suffer from paralyzing insufficiencies of national will, internal cohesion, material resources, or external appeal. These insufficiencies make them forego any meaningful regional foreign policy or else make them seek a common regional denominator with weaker countries as either an alternative or a preliminary to uncommon regional dominance. For the moment, America's imperial policy should be to keep open the various options which could lead to something more than elementary order, while at the same time she must continue to uphold such order as exists. The means for the latter involve the maintenance of access, aid, and intervention.

Access is a procedural requisite of order closely related to the structure of power. We have already indicated what kind of access we are concerned with: it is access to local balances or hierarchies of power and influence, which, while it obtains, avoids the need for reopening a closed door with massive force. So conceived, access shares with power the quality of a means so fundamental as to constitute a proximate goal, the irreducible object of the statecraft of an imperial power. The term "access" is conveniently broad; it stresses the basic condition for doing something deemed positive with the least possible exertion. The kinds of things that can be done, the goals beyond the proximate goal, will largely depend on the conditions and the costs of access. If access comes easily, involving little organized opposition, but is nonetheless subject to long-term threats, as in Latin America, the threats may stimulate creative efforts to resolve them. If access is strongly contested, as in the rimlands of Southeast Asia, it will be uneconomical and often impossible to do more than secure and maintain it. But, paradoxically, if the securing of contested access is not just a matter of force, efforts to secure the means may well entail promotion of the higher ends, like welfare and liberties, however much execution may be warped by the immediate purpose at hand. Conversely, where access is easy and unthreatened, there may be most of the time little incentive to employ resource and resourcefulness. Access and the requisites for securing it are thus both elastic and dynamic factors, interacting with local conditions and reflecting in any one place the general purpose of the power seeking it.

While the United States wishes to play a world role, access to key areas is essential. But no single technique is indispensable for securing or consolidating access. In contemporary conditions, neither military nor political access necessarily calls for permanent bases or continuous presence of the imperial power in more than a few strategic places. It will more generally require the existence of local forces and interests ready and able to give support and impart some legitimacy to American action, including intervention. This will, in turn, require, especially in doubtful and thus crucial cases, that local actors can proceed on the assumption of predictable American involvement in conditions which are grossly specifiable in advance. Next to predictability, access will be fostered by the impression of impartiality, an absence of a priori bias vis-à-vis local parties. Such impartiality must be steadily practiced even if it is not readily believed in by those with past or present grievances. It was not by accident that an earlier world power, Great Britain, committed to a regional balance of power in Europe, prided itself on not having any permanent friends but only interests, hopefully related to the overarching interest in orderly change. To be in consequence perceived as "perfidious" by one's would-be friends or declared enemies is something to be borne with equanimity. America's testing as a predictable imperial power has been most severe in Southeast Asia; as an even-handed one, in the Middle East.

Thirdly and ideally, access and the local conditions for securing access will be made easier by display of the capacity for asserting influence in a way which is both unprovocative and relatively undestructive. These requirements must be regarded as ideal, if only because they will often be difficult or even impossible to satisfy and may even be mutually contradictory. American action in South Vietnam has been deliberately kept within limits to avoid provoking either Russia or China; it has been as a result more destructive for the South Vietnamese than it might have been. Conversely, the prompt and even precipitate landing of American marines in Santo Domingo was provocative with respect to Latin American principles of nonintervention and constituted a deliberate challenge to Castroism in Cuba and the hemisphere; yet it was relatively nondestructive of both material goods and political values (discounting the automatic criticisms of all United States action in the western hemisphere).

I have used the terms "relative" and "ideal" in connection with the destruction wrought in the pursuit of access. The destruction in South and North Vietnam becomes more bearable when one regards the war not as a defense of South Vietnam or of the United States, but as an increasingly symbolic contest, with both global and long-range significance for the cause of order and therefore the degree and kind of peace in the world at large. Suffer as they do and must, the peoples of Vietnam are not the first or the last small people to render such a service to the larger commonweal.

Another significant, though not the decisive, instrument for promoting access is material and especially economic aid. I have little to add on this subject to what I wrote almost a decade ago.[2] The stuff of foreign aid and its specific objectives will doubtless continue to vary as the United States advances in technological and other skills and—freed from the constraints of an apparently close contest with the Soviet Union— can more frequently direct its concerns to more enduring political achievements on the part of the recipients. The principles, basic techniques, and conditions of requisite political control and military underwriting will, how-

[2] *The New Statecraft: Foreign Aid in American Foreign Policy* (Chicago: University of Chicago Press, 1960).

ever, remain much the same as they were in the 1950s. Politically administered foreign aid remains useful as one element in the dialectic of political development. And it is also useful as a means for penalizing disruptive activities. In other words, the chief task of foreign aid is to promote order, which will not always take care of itself in the short run, rather than progress, which either will occur in the long run without outside interference or will fail to materialize at all.

There have been growing doubts about foreign aid on the part of some earlier supporters. Recently, skepticism has been intensified by the tendency for aid to generate commitments that lead to involvements like Vietnam. If anyone overlooked such possibilities from the outset, he has only himself to blame. The lagging support for foreign aid actually exemplifies a much wider problem. There is an extreme proneness to eventual paralysis on the part of those who assess international action by the ideal yardstick of their vision of a placid new world. An expression of this attitude is found in the continuing and growing clamor for multilateral foreign aid, which represents one more instance of the desire to escape from foreign politics while nominally remaining in it—an attitude first manifested in American foreign policy with Wilson's advocacy of the League of Nations. It was then hoped that through a depoliticized collective security system the United States could act as leader in maintaining international order while remaining insulated from the more taxing aspects of the enterprise. Except perhaps where such vast schemes are disguises for national action, they depend on everyone doing his duty.

So far they have ended with little more than lip service to the ideal, which often amounts to a kiss of death for both the ideal and the more practical alternative approaches.

The third and most portentous instrument for upholding elementary order is intervention, already dealt with implicitly in much that precedes. The *mot d'ordre* here is, of course, discriminating intervention. But while discrimination is a matter of the doer's tact in concrete circumstances, a commentator can merely differentiate and distinguish. I shall offer observations on three distinctions: between multilateral and unilateral intervention; between what I shall call demonstrative intervention and locally determined intervention; and between overt and covert intervention.

An imperial power cannot commit itself to the multilateral mode in intervention as a matter of more than highly conditional preference. The guiding principle of action ought to be the relative capacity by one or the other mode to control the interventionist instrument and to promote its objective. To say this is to indicate that the mode employed ought not merely reflect the frustrations of the alternative mode. In a cyclic rhythm of preference, one might resort to essentially unilateral intervention in Vietnam in reaction to multilateralism in the Congo; or, vice versa, after or in the middle of Vietnam insist on multilateralism in the Middle Eastern crisis. Nor ought one to seek an escape from choice into preference for the multilateral form with unilateral content, as a matter of either convenience or principle. Multilateralism as disguise will always be tempting and possible for a great power with leverage, as shown in Korea and, to a lesser extent, in Vietnam; it should be restored to only when multilateralization does not forfeit in efficacy and sense of direction what it gains in presumed legitimation.

At present it is still easier for the United States to be multilateral in the company of lesser or client states than in association with the Soviet Union or the middle powers such as Britain, France, or Japan. But, if easier to stage, disparate multilateralism will be even more difficult to administer than the collective great power interventionism of the nineteenth century. It is in the nature of a salient imperial power to be perceived by lesser states as needing restraint by way of nonparticipation or obstruction more than as needing assistance and legitimation, and to be regarded as a fit object of blackmail by way of denial or conditional bestowal of support. In such circumstances, it will be up to the imperial power to choose coolly among strictly unilateral and isolated intervention, passively supported and mandated unilateral intervention, and genuinely multilateral intervention.

Leaders of the newer and weaker countries in particular have become less doctrinaire in their attutudes toward interventionism. Their concerns have become more variegated, as opposition to western colonialism ceases to preoccupy them so exclusively. Consequently, the imperial power will be increasingly able to choose its type of intervention in the light of fairly realistic nonparticipant attitudes, which will vary in nature and degree depending on the form of intervention. In choosing the form, the imperial power could also bargain with the nonparticipants, challenging them to provide an alternative to unilateral intervention or to support (or oppose) American action with deeds as a condition of regard for their viewpoints.

This is not to say that objectivity and capacity to act meaningfully for one's interests are widespread today, but that they ought to be encouraged among both the underdeveloped small countries and the middle powers of Europe and Asia. The latter have been trying to engage in great-power diplomacy in Southeast Asia and the Middle East by means of good offices and through offerings of aid. Yet the different, sporadic, and opportunistic uses that the super- and minipowers have for the middle powers have not added up to a functional utility for the middle powers that could serve as a substitute for responsible and effective use of real power. Nor can the conjunction of a favorable international constellation and the charismatic leadership of a Nehru, Tito, or de Gaulle lastingly insure influence. Although the French *force de frappe*, for instance, has sufficed to support a potentially beneficial role in Europe, where much can be achieved through skillful diplomacy,[3] meaningful French influence in Asia and Africa is likely to depend in the long run on a well-trained and mobile *force d'intervention*. Even India discovered this in the last days of Prime Minister Nehru. In the aftermath of the Suez fiasco, there has been some recrudescence in the use of military power by France and Great Britain in their narrowing colonial or postcolonial orbits. But no wider role for existing or developing capabilities has apparently been defined by the French, while the British have taken steps in the opposite direction by deciding to dismantle their

[3] This agrument is developed in my *Europe Ascendant* (Baltimore: The Johns Hopkins Press, 1964).

presence east of Suez. The mobile forces of middle powers will, however, eventually have to be available for more demanding performances than to invade a Goa or to cover a retreat from empire by crushing minor revolts in Africa or Arabia. It is doubtful that peremptory ceasefire orders and problematical peacekeeping operations under United Nations auspices, divorced from the rights and wrongs of parties, are an adequate long-term substitute for, say, armed mediation by relatively disinterested powers, an old-fashioned and recently much neglected diplomatic institution. One reason is that the readiness of the truly small states to take part in U.N. peacekeeping may well be on the wane, as internationally activist leaders in new states are replaced by more inward-oriented elites.

The United States can adopt a harder line on intervention, reflecting postcolonial realities, not only as a matter of power but also of principle. Unilateral intervention is not intrinsically inferior to multilateral intervention. In terms of public morality, the controlling aspects are the justice and the proportionality of the intervention and the disinterestedness of the intervening party. In these respects, the unilateral intervention of the United States in the Dominican Republic, for instance, compares favorably with the African component of multilateralism in the United Nations intervention in the Congo. There is more to it, though. The most frequent and only feasible multilateralism has been somewhat fictitious because the United States supplied the logistical and financial wherewithal. Yet it is a cardinal tenet of ethics that too great a gap between norm and act will degrade the norm rather than elevate the act. In this respect at least, South Vietnam has compared favorably with Korea.

The practical criterion of politic interventionism is one of efficacy, broadly conceived. In this respect, unilateral intervention will often be preferable in terms of the force required and the amount of destruction caused. It can be speedier than multilateral intervention, which may take more than American cargo planes to get it going. British and French interventions in their former colonial dependencies, and the combined American-Belgian intervention in the Congo, compare favorably in this respect with the United Nations intervention in the same country. The time advantage for unilateralism is not, of course, unconditional. It will be lost if unilateral intervention is slow in materializing out of respect for the multilateralists and their voting power in the United Nations or the United States and in deference to the politician's maxim that things have to get worse before one can start making them better.

Apart from technical efficiency, there is the broader political efficacy and expediency in unilateral intervention. It can be less disruptive not only in its narrow locus but also its wider circumference, thereby minimizing hostilities. Since local neighbors tend to feel more strongly or intensely about one another than they do about a remote and exalted great power, participation of neighbors in interventionist forces is apt to strain and poison relations even with those who have profited by a multilateral intervention. Lumumba's political friendship with his patron Nkrumah, and the new Congo's with the would-be successor to the Ghanian empire, would not have long survived a successful United Nations intervention, and least of all an all-African óne.

The preceding considerations and a related one—the magnitude of odium and trouble for the United States—are applicable to the recent Middle Eastern crisis. The United States chose to abide by the injunctions of the more consistent among the anti-unilateralists; it held out for multilateral action and abstained from opening up the strait of Tiran. Yet it is the latter course which in all probability would have thwarted the extremists on both sides. Instead, Nasser, with little latitude for improvisation, sought salvation in switching the prefabricated anti-American propaganda from an anticipated American action (sailing through the strait) to an invented one (flying in from the sea). He did so for the same reason for which he had probably hoped for the limited, unilateral American action as the least of several evils: one can bow to a great power and go on living in an upright posture; one cannot bend without breaking before a presumably equipowerful enemy-neighbor. In the absence of American intervention, Israel was given both an incentive and an opportunity for far-reaching offensive action. And the Soviet Union was spared yet another humiliation and could capitalize on that of the Arabs to improve its position in the Eastern Mediterranean. It did not have to seek improvement as a matter of give and take through a great power concert or confrontation. Altogether, the cause of peace and stability in the Middle East has not been much advanced. The presumed gains for stability from the unintended conjunction of Israeli action and American inaction may prove as ephemeral as did the presumed gains for peace from the subsequent displays of Arab moderation, calculated to put Israel in the wrong and make the United States act after all, if only diplomatically and against Tel Aviv.

The moral is simple: the imperial power must on occasion act like the lion in order to perform the function of the lamb; it must take onto itself and absorb the individual frailties and reciprocal hostilities of the weak. It must be prepared to act as the lightning rod, which prevents fires, and not only as the fireman who extinguishes those fires that were not or could not be prevented. The immediate consequence of such action is apt to be locally impeded access in parts of a region; in the long run, however, access will expand with expanding authority and prestige.

Another distinction to be made is between broadly demonstrative and locally determined intervention. By the first I mean intervention directed to ends which transcend, and are intended to transcend, the strictly local theater. This type of intervention serves as a demonstration of a wider interest and is addressed to other actors in comparable situations elsewhere. It is the wider object which will determine the utility and the form of the intervention; the opposite is true of situations which lack wider significance and which are the object of a locally required and determined intervention. It is in the nature of an imperial power that most of its interventions will be of the demonstrative kind, while the critics of unilateral imperial intervention will treat and assess most interventions purely in local terms.

Two conspicuous recent American interventions illustrate these distinctions. The intervention in

Santo Domingo does so even more strikingly than that in Vietnam, and both illustrate the crucial issue of timing. Insofar as the United States intends to demonstrate its readiness to act to a wider audience it may wish to act "precipitately," not only to protect itself against local surprises, but also to show that it will not be diverted by the disguises of others or delayed by seeking them for itself. Acting in this way will hopefully economize interventionist force and maximize interventionist effect; the opposite can result from prolonged delay.

The intervention in Vietnam has been demonstrative in an additional, and key, respect. It was intended to demonstrate not only readiness to act but also capacity to act with effect at a particularly strong sector of the adversary front. Only direct involvement by the two communist great powers might seem to be still harder to deal with than the North Vietnam-Vietcong combination supported by both, but it would also provide the United States with a more than offsetting additional facility for counteraction. Capacity to deal with the Vietnamese combination effectively would clearly demonstrate capacity to do likewise or better in other situations (as in Bolivia) and might help avoid the need to supply the proof again and again, at least on the level of overt violence. Similarly, the responses to onslaughts in North Korea and on Quemoy and Matsu more than proved American capacity to deal with an attack on Taiwan and with any other direct challenge by Chinese military power. The result was the verbal bellicosity and actual timidity in Chinese policy, which has since been invoked to controvert the need for American action in Vietnam. A similar point can be made in regard to other weak spots, such as Berlin, where the apparent readiness to fight did more to defend the frontier between East and West than if the readiness had been displayed in the Dardanelles, or in another strategic area more advantageous to the West.

Finally, the desire to show fidelity to allies who are suffering the consequences of their commitment is also a legitimate ground for demonstrative intervention where, in strictly local terms, "objective" grounds for it may be doubtful or even absent. The prestige of the United States in the Middle East or elsewhere was not increased by its failure to punish the brutal elimination of its special allies in Iraq in 1958. Failure to succor an ally in one place increases the pressure to act elsewhere to avoid the impression of consistent default. It is, therefore, dangerous to avoid proving fidelity in places where the cost of doing so appears to be relatively low.

The purpose of demonstration may require not only that the intervention be unilateral, so that it may be swift and spectacular, but also that it be overt. The question whether to camouflage or flaunt one's intervention is hard to assess in the abstract. To demonstrate skill in dealing covertly with disorder is not without value. This is true especially when dealing with actors who pride themselves on their capacity to work secretly. Such considerations would justify whatever role the United States had in the successful liquidation of the Guevara rebellion in late 1967 in Bolivia, and they explain the less successful effort to stay under cover, at least formally, in Cuba in 1961. Likewise, covert intervention in Iran, in the early 1950s, in opposition to the Mossadegh-Tudeh phenomenon, can be vindicated in local terms. It can be construed as an attempt to avoid revealing the loyalists as helpless without outside backing, and as a means to permit the Soviet Union to look the other way, as it may be anxious to do whenever its own covert support proves inadequate.

Yet covert intervention cannot be elevated to a preferred mode of action by an imperial power interested in world order. First, as in the Bay of Pigs fiasco, the very magnitude of the apparently intolerable disorder may be such as to render the efficacy of a covert intervention more than doubtful. Where the outcome is very problematic, covert intervention ought to be avoided. As the case of Cuba showed, a conservative and order-maintaining power cannot withdraw from such an operation without suffering great loss in prestige. Moreover, overt intervention is apt to insure more effective control over its beneficiaries and enable as well as compel the United States to press for remedial action after repression. The overt intervention in the Dominican Republic compares favorably in this regard with the earlier covert intervention in Guatemala. The final and most basic argument against covert intervention in defense of order is one of political morality. It rests on the belief that the commitment to uphold certain minimum standards of behavior by others limits the license in degrading them oneself.

IV. ANTI-INTERVENTIONISM AND IMPERIAL CONSCIOUSNESS

We now turn to the presently dominant attitudes toward foreign affairs in America. Traditionally, the range of attitudes has been covered by isolationism, imperialism, and internationalism. The prefix "neo" can be added nowadays at once conveniently and confusingly. The contending viewpoints can more usefully be reduced to two emphases, interventionist and anti-interventionist. The two viewpoints differ in their assessment of particular cases of intervention, in their underlying premises, and in their understanding of some key institutions and phenomena of international politics.

A succinct description of the contending schools would be difficult and not very revealing. There are wide differences among individual anti-interventionists, especially regarding the degree of their underlying commitment to internationalism as against isolationism. The interventionists differ, for their part, in the degree of their conscious commitment to an imperial role that entails recurrent interventions against communist and noncommunist agents of disorder alike. A fair idea of the "real" scope of both anti-interventionism and interventionism emerges most clearly from attitudes to past instances of intervention and from specific illustrations of principles to be applied in the future.

In retrospect we see that anti-interventionists opposed America's part in the resistance to China's attack on Quemoy and Matsu in the late 1950s just as unequivocally as they have since opposed action in South Vietnam; we find them equally opposed to intervention in Lebanon and in Santo Domingo. Some interventions are forever condemned, like the intervention in Guatemala; others are retroactively exonerated, even by convinced anti-interventionists, after history has proven their utility, if only because they put a critical issue on ice. Thus the Quemoy-Matsu intervention—which, like that in Vietnam, was originally regarded as fraught with excessive risks—has since assumed the halo of supreme virtue, that of successfully opposing a great power at the point of its greatest relative strength . . . and revealing its weaknesses. The action in Korea is now largely uncontested. As one of the causes and precedents for intervention on the Asian mainland, it may, however, come to suffer guilt by association with Vietnam or with a second Korean war. At present, the intervention in Korea can still be justified in anti-interventionist terms as a defense of Japan directly and the West indirectly against an expansionist Soviet Union. Moreover, it is possible not only to justify but also to idealize the Korean action by virtue of its association with the United Nations and the collective security principle. The action in the Congo, except for the humanitarian Stanleyville intervention in 1964, has been redeemed by the same collectivist token. The reaction to intervention in Cuba had been negative or ambiguous up to the point when the occurrence of a direct threat from the Soviet Union resolved doubts and rehabilitated the victors in the missile crisis from earlier charges of fumbling.

As regards prescriptions for the future, few points seem to emerge. Before World War II, the only compelling cause for American intervention outside the Western Hemisphere would seem to have been acute danger to the survival of Great Britain in the face of a threat from Germany. Western Europe as a whole, whenever conspicuously threatened by Soviet Russia, has succeeded to Britain's privileged position more recently. In Asia, feeble interventionist sentiments were previously aroused in the most isolationist of breasts by infringements of the American image of pre-Communist China. A stronger interventionist impulse is now dedicated, even by the anti-interventionists, to a Japan evolving in something like the American image and, secondarily and perhaps decreasingly, to India. Readiness to intervene for Japan or India is unlikely to be tested as long as the anti-interventionists are correct in their present estimate of Mao's China, which makes of it something like Mussolini's Italy between the wars—a vociferous but largely inoffensive claimant to the mantle of empire.

The anti-interventionists' propensity to intervene is weakest in regard to the Middle East and Africa, mainland Southeast Asia, and remoter parts of Latin America. A prima facie case for American intervention in those areas would exist only in the improbable event that regional instability seemed about to result in a major and direct accretion to Soviet or Chinese power. Even then, however, the only really conclusive criterion (direct threat to American security) is not seen as necessarily applicable, since power accretions in strategically secondary areas would not be decisive. In theory at least noninterventionism grows upon itself. The noninterventionist achieves fulfillment when he pronounces even the intervention of Great Britain in 1914 for either Belgian neutrality or the balance of power to have been unwise.[1]

Underneath superficial agreements and disagreements over the legitimacy of specific interventions lies the more important difference in premises. One premise concerns the nature of a society's material and moral resources for engagement, at home and abroad. The anti-interventionists believe that these resources are fixed and that allocations to domestic and international purposes are therefore competitive: The resources and energies which are spent abroad will be missing at home in the short run; the war on the Vietcong undercuts the war on poverty; to try to prevent the forcible unification of Vietnam is to defeat the peaceful integration of the Negro.

The pro-imperial emphasis, which is diametrically opposed, holds that the society's fund of resources is dynamic over a politically significant period of time; the resources and energies which are mobilized for action abroad are held to generate new and additional possibilities for simultaneous or subsequent domestic development. The

[1] See Edmund Stillman and William Pfaff, *Power and Impotence* (New York: Random House, 1966), p. 160n. The reasons for this judgment can only be divined. They apparently rest on the belief that an Imperial Germany dominant on the continent would have been a more manageable adversary or condominial partner for an undiminished Great Britain than a nazified defeated Germany proved to be for an England weakened by World War I. The belief is debatable, if not necessarily false.

expanded, imperial theater provides new roles and possibilities for adjusting competing claims; the condition is that the external effort must be pursued with skill and with lucidity about its meaning. Thus expansiveness of Britain and France abroad in the late nineteenth century, and even of Soviet Russia in the Khrushchev era, coincided with the expansion of both resources and individual and group liberties at home. On the other hand, failure and frustration abroad affect the domestic scene adversely. The shrinkage of the international positions of France beginning with the 1930s and of England after World War II was attended by internal stress from intensified social or ethnic group demands.

The most potent extensible resources are the leaders' belief in themselves and the confidence they inspire among the led. On the part of the led, the key resources are their skills and stamina, as well as their readiness to render service and ration social grievance or economic desires. The critical shrinkage of resources is not due to external expenditure of treasure. It follows rather from the constriction of intangibles (such as identification of minority groups with the larger community and the community's élan and sense of purpose) under external pressures and unresisted internal pretensions and demands. The imperial advocate will have to admit, of course, that concessions to particular groups and interests can on occasion be most easily wrested from thwarted imperial elites, as in Tsarist Russia, or from their successors, as in Germany after World War I. But he will add that such concessions are unlikely to mark a step forward for the community as a whole, or even to produce an acquisition which may be long and peacefully enjoyed by the recipients.

The relation and the difference between the above assumptions become more significant when we add the second and third set of assumptions. The second set bears on the anti-interventionist notion of defensive enclave, as against purposeful involvement. The quantity which, in this respect, is deemed to be fixed or dynamic is not the nation's resource. It is the total environment, international and national. Advocates of military or political enclaves, widely or narrowly defined, do not regard the environment as decisively affected by the scope and intensity of one's action. They seem to assume that the enemy will maintain a steady and acceptable level of pressure, and that the friendly or neutral states will pursue positive policies and favorable balances of power, whether the American posture is active or inactive. On the basis of this assessment, the enclave strategist prescribes withdrawal into fortified positions as a means of liquidating an overcommitment on the Asian mainland and, in the larger theater, a limitation of commitments to a few positions vital for the deployment of America's pre-eminent sea and air power.

The interventionist view is different. A power once paramount or salient cannot, in the absence of some new source of elementary order, withdraw behind a smaller perimeter and avoid adverse reactions. The reaction can be the flight into opportunistic self-reliance by former protégés or a thrust forward into ever more aggressive self-affirmation by those formerly cowed or checked by superior power. The situation today is one of diffuse, ambiguous, and decentralized pressures (as contemporary anti-interventionists are the first to argue) rather than one of a clear and compelling common threat to noncommunist countries. In such a situation, the proponent of the imperial role would not dare base policy on the theory that retreat under pressure from advanced positions would prove that the United States is realistic and therefore more reliable; or that it would induce other states to become more cooperative or more self-dependent as defenders of some order compatible with the American ideal.

The domestic implications of the controversy over Vietnam are equally important. The key domestic issue is the racial crisis. There is an interdependence between affirmation of American prestige and power vis-à-vis Hanoi and its allies and the prospect for a semi-orderly integration of American society in the face of Black Power. In the last resort, whatever order exists in the United States depends on the government's known will and ability to deal firmly with hostile force. A collapse of this reputation abroad would strengthen the appeal and increase the credibility of domestic advocates of violence as a safe and profitable way to "racial equality." Any administration conspicuously thwarted abroad would be bound to have the greatest difficulty in dealing with domestic crises. The consequence of default in the exercise of the imperial role might very well be a Second American Revolution for the "independence" of a hitherto "colonized" group. An internationally discredited American government might have as much trouble mastering the second revolution as a similarly handicapped British government had with the first, or as the Russian regime had with the revolutions of 1905 and 1917.

Historical analogies of this kind may seem inapplicable to the United States. Also, new potentialities for managing domestic conflict—plus compulsions for avoiding international entanglements —may seem inherent in expansive industrial societies. Yet the traditional wisdom that encourages the display of fortitude wherever most feasible or least painful cannot be fully ignored.

Our discussion of the government's will and prestige is related to a third set of assumptions that divide the debators over imperial involvement. These assumptions have to do with the stability of the people's will. Popular attitudes cannot be expected to remain constant during a strenuous foreign war and in the face of a peace that would not justify the costs of the war, especially if a still more costly "internal war" were to follow. There is less genuine difference on this subject between politically sophisticated interventionists and anti-interventionists than on the other two, although there is some on the practical implications.

Faced with a war in which "costs" seem to exceed possible "gains," anti-interventionists have advocated a no-victory peace as a formula for extricating the United States from a deepening international involvement. In their anxiety to have done with agony, they have tended to de-emphasize one of statecraft's more tragic near-impossibilities: that of achieving a genuine no-victory peace relative to initial objectives and to the effort expended. Such a peace may be remotely possible, if at all, only between two or more states of comparable standing, especially when these states become less concerned about their ambitions than about still another country. Or a no-victory peace may turn into a truce with far from satisfactory consequences. A festering Korean issue may yet confirm this point in our time. No more reassuring on this score is the nearest thing to a no-victory settlement of a major war known to modern European diplomacy, the peace of 1748. It settled neither the German issue nor the colonial issue and the war of Austrian succession was resumed after eight years to last another seven. The Peace of Vienna was made in 1815 only after France was clearly defeated twice in succession and the Treaty of Ghent, terminating the War of 1812, was concluded under the impression of the clear military preponderance of Great Britain over the United States. Neither of these preconditions is present in Vietnam in early 1968. Moreover, neither of the two peace settlements did much more than restore the formal conditions prevailing before the wars began. This would hardly be regarded as a no-victory settlement by either the United States or its adversaries, depending on whether 1959 or 1965 are taken as determining for the purpose of restoration.[2]

[2] These disputed instances are cited by J. W. Fulbright, *The Arrogance of Power* (New York: Random House, 1967), p. 183. The alleged magnanimity of British vis-à-vis the Americans in the Ghent treaty-making and after can hardly be invoked as a model either. It was a compound, with a changing balance of components as the century grew older, of condescension, concern over other dangers (the Holy Alliance and, later, Russia and Germany), and confident expectation that underlying affinities would tell in the long run. Instead, the real situation facing the British and the French is worth remembering. It is best illustrated by their inability to maintain an earlier Napoleonic peace, that of Amiens, which, while

Always difficult to achieve, a no-victory peace may be impossible between such disparate adversaries as the United States and the coalition of Hanoi and the National Liberation Front. It would depend on Hanoi breaking with China and its own regional expansionism, or the NLF breaking with both China and Hanoi. In any other event, the postwar participation and presence in Vietnamese politics and security matters of either the NLF or the United States (or even the United Nations) would be largely fictitious and temporary—a face-saving device which would deceive no one, rather than a reassuring safeguard against violations of the new order.

A way out of the dilemma has been sought in proposals to neutralize Vietnam or Southeast Asia as a whole, perhaps in conjunction with a governmental role for the NLF. Yet international safeguards could hardly guarantee a coalition's survival. And the neutralization precedents—Switzerland, Belgium, and, presently, Austria—point to preconditions which can be secured in Southeast Asia only by continued assertion of American military power. Neutralizing a country was in the past possible only at the end of prolonged or recurrent contests, not at their beginning or midpoint. It depended on continued military or political impact on the neutralized area by ideally three outside powers or blocs. It was possible only after the neu-

---

favoring the expansionist power, was still a peace of genuine compromise. The reasons for this inability, having to do with reciprocal fears as well as ambitions, are infinitely more applicable to America's present relations with any one expansionist Communist power than either Anglo-French relations after Leipzig and Waterloo or Anglo-American relations after New Orleans.

tralized country had shot its bolt in history as a first rate military power and was anxious to remove itself from stress, a condition which applies to a Laos but not to North Vietnam. And, of course, neutralization worked only for countries constituting cohesive communities. Only the requirement of three powers underwriting local neutrality might be met in Southeast Asia. For this to happen, however, China would have to agree to neutrality and both the Soviet Union and the United States would have to remain concerned, powerful in the area, and distinct in policy.

There is a last point to be made. Neutralization is not necessarily a no-victory solution; and it need not lastingly favor the winning side. Neutralizing independent Belgium was a victory for Britain over France, the neighboring power with annexationist desires. It was also a victory for Britain and France over the conservative Eastern Powers, including Prussia, which favored continued union of Belgium with the Netherlands. But, in the end, Belgian independence and neutrality came to favor Germany over the western powers by inhibiting French national defense in two world wars. In prevailing conditions, effective neutralization of "democratic" South Vietnam along with communist North Vietnam and the rest of Southeast Asia would be a success for the remote United States, provided it retained political access to the area, insofar as neutralization represented a barrier to expansion by indigenous China. But a neutral Southeast Asia might in due course complicate America's task of dealing with a strengthened China which could violate or circumvent the neutralized rimlands.

The debate over American foreign policy which has boiled up as a result of the Vietnam war has been fraught with conflicting affirmations and conceits. The debate, which actually predates Vietnam, cannot be resolved soon in favor of either side, before or after the outcome of the war is known. One of its most confusing aspects is that there frequently seems to have been agreement on the basic trends and guidelines of American policy when they are stated in generalities, but great discord when the effort is made to implement these policies. In the interests of clarification and explication I have singled out six controversial issues or aspects of the debate for discussion; there are others, but the six I have chosen represent areas of fundamental disagreement between the interventionists and the anti-interventionists.

Issue number one concerns the relation of internal and external effort. All are in favor of coming to grips with social and urban problems in the United States. But whereas the internationalists of yesterday were all for large-scale foreign economic aid, the liberal anti-interventionists have more recently been comparing the billions allegedly wasted abroad and those presently needed for domestic programs. In doing so they seem to forget that a domestic "giveaway," like the foreign expenditure, would not have the desired effect unless it occurred within the right political framework; unless economic aid is matched with authoritative administration, compassion with control, commitment to progress with capacity to foster order, and commitment to order with a capacity to control and resolve internal conflict.

It may be that, in the very short run, even a rich nation like the United States has to determine its priorities when allocating resources either for a war on the Vietcong or on poverty. But it is doubtful that this dichotomy applies to the really crucial underlying issues of social and political integration of a dynamic body politic. Social integration in conditions of order and an expansive foreign policy are actually interdependent in the longer run. Generally considered, the degree to which it is harder to predict, control, and re-create conditions and events in the international arena than in the realms of domestic policy will promote foreign-policy activism and interventionism on the part of states which can at all have an active foreign policy. This will offend those who resent the natural and contrary tendency to inertia in domestic politics. But, a failure to accommodate policy to the special needs of the foreign arena is apt, sooner or later, to lead to crises blamed on prior inaction which will adversely affect conditions in the domestic arena as well.

There is a more basic aspect to the interdependence of domestic and foreign policies. A successful past foreign policy, like America's, which helped create the conditions of an expanding body politic beset with unavoidable competition among established and rising group interests, will acquire a momentum of its own. Such momentum will have to be maintained if peaceful adjustment of internal group conflicts is to be facilitated over time by the continuing expansion of outlets and targets for political attention and controversy. If there can be too little concern with internal issues, there can be an overconcentration on them; the dispersal of interest and resources is often preferable to their polarization and confrontation.

Any active, far-reaching foreign policy will go

beyond the "bread" of foreign aid and the "games" of U.N. debates and cultural diplomacy. It will involve armed action which, once it assumes the form of protracted war, will unavoidably create the impression of conflict between socio-political integration and foreign-policy intervention. The impression is false. Whereas a growing state is typically drawn into expansive foreign action by conflicts involving the international balance of war-making power, at a later stage such a state will be more typically led to perpetuate an expansive policy as a condition of peacefully balancing the interests of relatively receding and advancing subjects of interest and power within the body politic itself. When this happens, and it is happening in and for the United States, national security as the principal motive and warrant for expansive foreign-policy action is superseded by national stability and cohesion. The two add up to something like national integrity when, next to the gratification of more prosaic drives and needs, one assigns a proper place to the satisfaction of the higher need for meaningful individual and collective political function, abroad as well as at home, and comes to terms with the fact that each arena attracts actors with a different (and potentially antagonistic) conception of worthwhile political action and thus, in the last resort, of the good life.

The crisis normally attending transition from a parochial to an imperial body politic, often in a frustrating first imperial war, reflects the difficulties implicit in reassessing the interrelation between domestic and external needs and efforts in the domain of action, and in effecting the switch from national security to national integrity in the domains of motivation and justification for action abroad. Without such re-evaluation, however, it is impossible to generate either the consent or the authority for adapting domestic group demands to external obligations. International obligations are denied validity as long as they are seen as obstacles to material satisfactions, hindering efforts to implement the obligations in such a way as to heighten their potential utility as an avenue and a precondition to a wider range of satisfactions. The debate and the contest are diverted from the valid and essential qualitative question of how to implement a recurrent constant of involvement to the quantitative question of how much to retain and discard of a presumably variable and optional commitment. The basic condition of implementing the imperial role in a sustained manner is to shield the critical and persistent foreign-policy modes from carping and changeable domestic moods. An updated organization of national power and public powers might conduce to that end. The legitimizing basis for a partial disconnection between domestic and foreign politics in a democratic society is the acceptance of the underlying interconnection between international and domestic stability in the longer run. For the public to accept recurrent external involvement, as an alternative to concurrent internal and external anarchy, is a vital condition to be fulfilled if the United States is to continue its evolution from a middle-class democracy to an imperial democracy multiracially structured, socially and economically mobile, and internationally responsible.

In connection with the war in Vietnam, the United States has been favored with two opportunities for making a major step in the crucial transition. After the first opportunity had been wasted in an inauspicious beginning, the second opportunity arose when interest in the war fell off with the beginning of "peace talks" and the shift of public concern to internal racial and social issues which, far from being caused by the war, had been exacerbated in the name of a progressively radicalized and partially discredited opposition to it. This opposition, the escalation of which paralleled the war's and created comparable problems of association and control for its originators, had been initially given sustenance by official actions designed to minimize external criticism and counteraction. A prematurely advertised quest for peace had implicitly disavowed the war's rationale in favor of the opponents' reasoning, while conditions for useful negotiations were undermined by failure to make a basic decision on the war's conduct. The United States did not generate in time a manifest capability for a discreet, protracted, and largely professionally fought type of war. Nor, when the politically motivated early delays and subsequent deterioration of the military situation reduced the practical value of the preferable mode, did the United States display the will and ability to destroy the enemy's nerve and support by means calculated to strengthen its own—giving, that is, the war a chance of becoming a patriotic war by investing it with the kind of risks and underwriting it with the kind of resources which belong to the species.

The second issue concerns the use and type of force. All are against wasteful and unnecessary use of force, at home and abroad. But whereas the early isolationists were against all involvement in foreign wars, the contemporary anti-interventionist, for the most part, is only against "undiscriminating" involvements. In practice these turn out to be all involvements that might or do prove to be onerous or dangerous. In so doing, the critics of intervention have forgotten that in the concrete case of Vietnam no responsible statesman could remain inactive in the expectation that the NLF would offset Hanoi, Hanoi offset China, and Thailand keep Cambodia in line, while India and Japan, in the longer run, stalemated one another and kept an increasingly vigilant and benevolent eye on all the rest. The contrary view holds that some wars may be necessary not only in principle but also in immediate fact, as long as commitments do not always deter but sometimes involve, do not always protect but sometimes provoke, in proportions which no one can confidently anticipate. The United States has fought in Vietnam in the late 1960s not only because it fought and established both a precedent and a position in Korea in the early 1950s but also because it did not want to fight in Laos in the early 1960s. It has fought the second Indochina war because it had entered into certain commitments in order to make up for not joining in the first.

The related question is that of the type of force employed. Here the anti-interventionist fears the straight line of escalation from conventional force, if applied extensively, to nuclear force. He has tended to forget or ignore the pressures for nuclear compensations for the failure to apply conventional weapons with effect.

The third issue concerns an alternative order, that of balanced power. All favor the progressive restoration of regional balances of power around the world in the hope that they will reduce or at least differentiate America's global involvements. The ideological forebears of many a contemporary anti-interventionist were almost to a man against the very idea of balances of power. Opposing American interventionism today, however, often means being for balance of power in theory; it means assuming its actual near-existence where there is no trace of it and fulminating against the side-effects of its apparent or potential reappearance in Europe. The tendency is to forget that even approximate balances would not spell the end of American exertions and might render them at times more delicate and difficult, not the least because such "balances" will tend to favor the locally expansive or expansionist powers, liable to oppress the lesser powers.

There are, moreover, more immediate difficulties with the neo-internationalist balance-of-power argument. To play an active role in a balance of power, a state must have both power and will. In Asia, local power is expected, by opponents of Vietnam, to increase sufficiently before China becomes a real threat. But there are few indications that Asia will soon develop countervailing power against China, as long as middle powers like Japan and India desist from developing conventional military power for regional use and nuclear deterrent power able to shield such use. Instead, the local states are likely to continue to base their security, with or without proper acknowledgment and counterperformance, on American military power, and on the nuclear deterrent balance between the two superpowers, which is presumed to compel them to prevent China from utilizing her nuclear capability for expansionist ends. For some time to come, any balance-of-power order in the third world is thus likely to be an appearance deriving substance, as long as it is untested, from two half-truths about two balancing performances. Both performances—one by local conventional military power, the other by global strategic power—are considered all the more reliable, the more the would-be beneficiaries —the United States in the first case and a middle power like India in the second—abstain from action, reducing their contingent exertions and costs on the strength of the presumed supplemental reactions of other powers.

Like international organization globally, most regional power and all regional balances must first be nurtured under the umbrella of superior power before the indigenous states can grow sufficiently to replace the sponsor. It is, therefore, at best premature for the United States to foster the balance of power in Asia against China by disengaging from the Asian mainland.

Next to power in importance is will. The will to play a role in balancing power is supposed to derive from local nationalisms. These will prevail over all other concerns, including the ties of shared communism, it is often argued, should it prove necessary for containment of China or any other local expansionists. The advocates of this assessment extend the notion of nationalism, noncommunist or communist, from postcontainment Europe to precontainment Asia as a substitute for American involvement, while they criticize those who would extend the containment concept (while modifying it) from Russia to China. The argument further asserts that containment in Asia is impracticable because the United States cannot find reliable allies there. This line of argument ignores the fact that containment was largely a one-man show in Europe as well in the most critical aspects and phases. In this respect, pre-de Gaulle France in Europe resembles today's France in Asia more than the ideal of a stalwart ally. Advocates of nationalism meet these protestations with the assertion that, while there is no reliable alliance-material in Asia, there are enough states sufficiently vital to do the containing on their own, only somewhat later. The removal or reduction of American power is held to be necessary to make these countries wake up to their responsibilities.

The riposte is not compelling. The sense of responsibility fed by nationalism is presumed to develop in opposition to China. But the call for American withdrawal is being issued along with the judgment that China is more threatened than threatening, that she seeks security and status rather than supremacy. It is as if American power had to be withdrawn so that China would be encouraged to show her real face, thus awakening local states to the sense of their real interests. This is a daring gamble, at the very best. Nor is this all. Local nationalism is supposed to develop in the wake of American withdrawal from areas surrounding a presently pacific and only verbally and internally violent China. Actually, such withdrawal is apt to atrophy any nascent Asian nationalisms or turn them inward to internecine conflicts, rather than make them into a basis for an Asian balance of power. There is a good if unpleasant reason for this. American interventionism serves the dual function of an irritant and a conveniently unacknowledged protector. It constitutes that vital component which, with luck, may progressively turn the Asian reeds of today into tomorrow's pillars of strength.

The fourth issue concerns a regional hierarchy of power. Many have come to think that a stable world order will have to comprise a special position in the different regions or subregions for the most resourceful local power or powers. Earlier internationalists condemned the very idea of spheres of influence, except perhaps where it took the form of the Monroe Doctrine. By contrast, many contemporary neo-internationalists or neo-isolationists have come to be sympathetic to such arrangements. They tend to equate the achievement of privileged position by one power with agreement on such position among all of the greater powers. In so doing they tend to forget that such spheres cannot be explicitly negotiated by the greater powers any more than they ought to be forcefully decreed for the lesser ones. If special responsibilities are to be unevenly distributed in the world without being or becoming exclusive and oppressive in any part of it, they must be so distributed in a lengthy process of great-power competition over and involving the lesser states. Such a competition must be informed by the vision of an interlocking system of preferential but still basically reciprocal access and influence by leading regional and extra-regional powers in central-eastern Europe just as in central or northern Africa, in Southeast Asia just as in Latin America.

The fifth issue concerns yet another institution of order, a great power concert. One may well look forward to the day when world order will rest on a global equivalent of a concert of stable and satiated powers. But, whereas earlier internationalists and isolationists alike rose up in horror against the idea of anything resembling a Holy Alliance, their descendants today speak readily of the concert of free nations or nuclear powers. They choose to forget that without a conducting power a concert is but a cacophony, and that if there is to be a band (let alone a concert), the powers must first work out their seating order and the allocation of instruments. This too will be more than a matter of a rational agreement amiably arrived at. Even the most efficacious concert involves a complicated interplay of conflict, containment, and compensation. As part of an ad hoc concert, multilateral intervention by great powers has many advantages over either unilateral intervention by one great power or its pseudomultilateral intervention in the company of smaller states. But it is unwise to suspend action until or unless one can enjoy the collaboration of one's peers. To do so would be to forget that most multilateral interventions on record, and there are not many, are the result of one great power's conspicuous readiness for intervention and of the other powers' reluctance to see it profit therefrom while they keep aloof.

The sixth, last, and perhaps most important issue concerns the ideological and racial sources of conflict and disorder. Most of us wish to attenuate the role of militant ideology in international politics and forestall the intensification of a racial substitute or complement. But when the critics of official policy deride the ideological justification of the Vietnam war in terms of a fight against Asian communism as both obtuse and obsolete, they are forgetting an important point: A government has to rationalize a military involvement somehow and the critics themselves have barred the route to an updated rationale by violently rejecting any idea of an ideologically neutral policing role for the United States. We must not, when contemplating official doctrines from the outside, take them too literally. An embarrassed government has stressed Asian or Chinese communism as a threat justifying involvement. But a resort to ideology may merely rationalize an exercise in omnipotence just as legalism rationalized an earlier condition of impotence. The vocabulary of the armed Johnson Doctrine of resistance to aggression in Southeast Asia has been aimed at the China of the 1960s; it need not be taken at face value any more than the rhetoric of an unarmed Stimson Doctrine of nonrecognition of territorial gains made by Japan at the expense of the China of the 1930s. In politics as in diplomacy words are still occasionally used to disguise thought and not always to make up for its deficiency.

There is a more important point to be made. Ideology as a controlling factor in international politics has never eroded as a result of avoiding conflicts in which ideology played a major role. Ideological erosion will occur more certainly if parties engage in active contests. They are then compelled to come face to face with the limited utility of ideology in mustering strength, finding or consolidating allied support, and defeating or repulsing an enemy. To enter into ideologically impure relationships and connections as a result may be deemed expediential and temporary; it will actually start an irreversible movement away from ideology toward pragmatic *Realpolitik*. Great contests tend to begin in an overstatement of ideal or ideological differences between the adversaries and then rather quickly become contests of territorial powers wanting the same thing—Italy, in the case of France and the Habsburgs, Indochina in that of Hanoi, China, and the United States. It would, therefore, have been remarkable if the Sino-American confrontation had begun otherwise. The confrontation will move one day beyond its over-ideologized beginning. But this will be the result of action rather than agitation, of expediency rather than exhortation.

To accelerate the erosion of an ideology like communism by forcing its proponents to come to terms with their Reason of State is not identical with relying on sentiments of nationhood to undermine communism as a universal force. To rely on nationalism against communism is to rely on an irrational and often expansionist ideology against a relatively rational one. This may be a poor remedy in areas where the combination of nationalism and underdevelopment is apt to lead to strife, racialism, and tribal separatism. It is hazardous for the United States to enter into an opportunistic alliance with an intrinsically unmanageable force in order to weaken an adversary which, while hard and resourceful, is at least structured in organization and calculating in action. Such an alliance is likely to lead to an impasse represented by unanswerable questions like the following: How will the United States deal with Vietnamese nationalism incarnated in Hanoi when Hanoi turns against Cambodia and Laos in the name of historic rights, rather than—or, as well as—against China on the grounds of historic grievances? Will the United

States then stand aside, relying on competing nationalisms to show which is the "better" because "stronger," just as successful resistance to communism is now deemed to be the function of superior democracy rather than a matter of superior combination of wile and will? There are some precedents in this matter. In the 1950s, for instance, the United States was invited and even tried for a while to attach American policy in the Near East to the then fresh nationalism of the young officers around Nasser. Had the alliance with Nasser been consummated, the Soviets might very well now have a single major ally in the Middle East, rebelling against belated American restraints on action against Israel or Saudi Arabia, rather than a host of weak and ambiguous clients.

The historical record is no more encouraging when we turn from nationalism as a weapon for destroying ideology to the anatomy of ideologically grounded revolutions. Such revolutions tend to reach a largely irreversible point of revulsion from puritanic zeal and terror in a conservative reaction exemplified by the events of the month of Thermidor in the French revolutionary model. But this process, far from being unaided, is rather closely related to foreign-policy pressures and opportunities, real or alleged. In the first phase, external hostility will intensify or at least justify internal extremism, which will in due course provoke self-defensive reaction by those anxious to save their skins and, incidentally, the body politic. Thus foreign pressures at the very least accelerate the reversion to something like moderation. In the second phase, the world outside will readily serve as a substitute target for the revolutionary drive.

The drive is endowed with re-acquired managerial efficacy; its outward redirection makes up for the "betrayal" of revolution at home. Although the outside world's pressure has a moderating impact on the revolution in the first phase, in the second phase its potential for perpetuating the remaining revolutionary élan is greater the less effective is its opposition. Weak opposition will tend to keep alive the contempt for the external world acquired in the period of revolutionary purity. The first phase of development, from terror to Thermidor, is represented by the Directoire in France, the transition from the Long to the Little Parliament in England, and the first Soviet collective leadership in post-Stalin Russia; the second phase is illustrated by the First Consul and Emperor, the Lord Protector, and the Chairman of the Presidium. Napoleon fulfilled the French Revolution abroad, Cromwell translated into offensive policy the puritanic hatred of Spain, and Khrushchev bestirred himself to spread socialism to many countries while humanizing it in its homeland. In the case of China, the combination of thermidor, thermonuclear weapons, and traditional hostility for the western barbarians, brought to fever heat by the revolution, might prove to be quite an explosive postrevolutionary compound in the absence of an awe-inspiring external power barrier.

Ideology has something in common with race, to the extent that both are matters of images and myths. If we are to keep the issue of racial differences from replacing or reinforcing the ideological issue as the one that dominates international politics, it will not be done by avoiding racially colored conflicts and racially mixed alignments.

The solution is not to let Asians fight Asians or Africans fight Africans—or else have only Negroes police rioting Negroes. It would be as hazardous to depend on the self-equilibrating dynamic of interracial animosities between Arab and black African, Malay or Annamite and Chinese, African and Asian, as it would be imprudent to depend on the conflict between Peking and Hanoi to determine regional influence. And it would be offensive to detach American concern from disorders in most of Asia and Africa, save for enclaves of strategic importance or cultural affinity, on the avowed or implied grounds that these areas do not have enough strategic value or local power to interest anyone but the local peoples.

American abstention which could be explained in this way is apt to create more serious alienation than would American involvement. The resentments which involvement creates are in any event a matter of waxing and waning sentiment, unfit to govern the grand strategy of a great power and unworthy of too much stress by those who oppose interventionism in the name of practicality. Rather than trying to avoid all resentments all the time, the United States government may have cause to arouse some now to forestall greater ones in the future. The United States did well when it first intervened in the Congo to protect whites in the face of a black rebellion in 1964 and then, in 1967, rendered assistance to the central government against white mercenaries when they became insubordinate.

The United States deserves praise when it involves itself locally in a way which scrambles the lines of both alignment and confrontation, acquires and keeps allies and protégés of all racial denominations, and thus forestalls two major dangers. The first is that, if left to themselves, indigenous regional powers will seek to reinforce their positions or temporarily reduce local rivalries by raising again the cry of racial exclusiveness—"Asia for the Asians," "Africa for Africans," or even "Latin America for the Latinos." Racially disguised regional supremacists in Asia such as Communist China (coming on the heels of Imperial Japan) would endanger inter-racial accommodation more than do the racial supremacists in South Africa and elsewhere.

The second of the two dangers is implicit not only in indigenous communism but also in much more elementary prototypes and conditions. If the necessary underpinning of occasional intervention against serious disorders were to falter, the whole delicate structure of what now is called the South-North relationship would be liable to collapse, especially in regard to development assistance. A widening development gap would be compounded with a widening stability gap which, together with other gaps, would release untold hostility toward the industrialized world. All the slave rebellions and class conflicts of the past would then appear as tame dress rehearsals for the ensuing alienation and conflict among the races.

The fact that the task of coping with the racial issue in the world at large has fallen mainly to the United States is the kind of accident which gives history a convincing semblance of meaning. In the shape of the United States, the moderating and mediating role has fallen to a people which is less of an inbred tribe than any other in existence. The United States is a society cosmopolitan in makeup and still free to become such in conduct, a country which is internally experiencing the global problem found in the interaction of different ethnic and racial groups at different levels of equality and felt worth. Diversity makes the United States more capable of performing global tasks in the long run because it constitutes a built-in incentive to continued concern. This is more important than the short-term handicap of internal crises resulting from the same diversity.

The relationship between multiracial makeup and world policy is, moreover, a two-way street. The United States can much more hopefully look toward a resolution of its racial problems if the issue, presently bottled up and polarized on the levels of community, state, and nation, can be dissolved, as it were, in a larger, multiracial framework of global dimension. The imperial approach to racial diversity is the only workable method so far on record; it is not to be discarded lightly before others prove practicable. Already, the role which imperial involvement can play in the national predicament is manifest on the high as well as the low levels of society. It is manifest whenever the Negro GI in Vietnam or the educated middle-class Negro in the American foreign-policy establishment experiences his identity as *Civis Americanus* with much greater self-assurance abroad than he can at home. A gain is realized whenever one or the other returns home with a sharpened sense of relative personal worth after rendering service and with a revised sense of group affinities after having experienced differentness from other nonwhite races. An imperial experience need not always have such ideal results.

Much depends on the opportunities the repatri-
ated servant of the imperial *patria* finds at home.
But few local, parochial experiences hold an equal
or higher potential.

V. CONCLUSION

It is too simple to believe that the way to achieve peace is to avoid war; the way to recover peace, to call for negotiation; the way to disarm, to merely discard armaments. To have peace, it is still necessary not only to prepare for war, but also on occasion to fight one; and to fight a war resolutely if one is to have a reasonably good and long peace. It may even be necessary to refuse to consider negotiation in order to make an arrogant adversary ready and anxious for it; to assert imperial power in order to make other strong nations ready to collaborate in a concerted and multilateral order; and to meet the dilemmas of ideology and race in international politics head on in order to prepare an escape from them.

We have reached the end of our argument. After so many questions, affirmations, and attempted refutations we could do worse than end on a note of qualified skepticism in one respect and qualified hope in another. The qualified skepticism concerns the anti-interventionist position. It is not all wrong, but its policy conclusions are premature on essential points. The anti-interventionists are prone to preach against an excess of zeal in foreign policy; yet they are the real zealots, heady with the success of American policies in the cold war, making too much of some desirable and by now widely acknowledged trends away from ideological rigidity and power polarity in international relations. They

111

seem prepared to run the risk of submerging these delicate incipient trends in. the turbulence that would result from the shrinkage of both involved American power and the expectations attached to that power and involvement. A major retrenchment of an active major power, however staged and camouflaged, will inevitably produce reactions— reactions which are hard to predict and not easy to control. Some positive reactions, in the domain of self-reliance, are possible; but many more negative repercussions, in the domain of expansion of rivals and defeatism of friends and dependents, are certain. Politics is, admittedly, the art of the possible; but it is first and foremost the hard labor of averting the highest evil before reaching out for the supreme good. The damage may well prove reparable if the shrinkage is temporary, the result of the withdrawal of shiftless power rather than the collapse of decayed power; this was the case when the fluctuating involvement was Britain's in the eighteenth and nineteenth centuries. But the cost of repairing the damage is commonly great, first for the international system and in due course for the leading nation itself.

After qualified skepticism comes qualified hope. If only the United States, its people and its leaders, could find in themselves the insight and the resolve to apply the weary wisdom of the ages while retaining the leavening dose of original innocence, they might start something genuinely new and authentically revolutionary in the affairs of man. Then, and only then, could we begin to move toward a world in which humane precept prevails over hoary precedent, a world in which the forces for choice could effectively counter the weight of necessity, because fundamental change would no longer be equated with disorder.

The challenge is great, but so is the price of failing without having really tried. Social disorientation and indifference to the larger issues of politics have often followed upon the loss of empire. They are, however, also the concomitants of having nothing worthwhile to do as a nation among nations. The Swedes had their Gustavus Adolphus and Charles XII before they had to fall back for international respect and national self-respect upon a Bernadotte and a Hammarskjold, under the protective safeguard of an imperial eagle hiding in the folds of the U.N.'s blue flag. The Germans are still not at peace with themselves, because they muffed all three of their efforts at empire. The French—perhaps unlike the British—can live with themselves and their past as long as they believe that an empire of the spirit, in the form of the French tongue and French-style diplomacy, may yet do duty for the lost empire of the sword. As for the United States, the range of options is narrowing at a rapid pace. Only one thing seems certain. Almost two centuries after the Founding Fathers acted with a premonition of imperial destiny for their new country, the greatest pages of American history are still those of its beginning.

The key for relating America's early anticipation of empire to her possible consummation is to be found in the two meanings of *imperium*: externally unrestricted rule, or sovereign independence; and restrictive rule for order, itself constrained by a higher law or an inward sense of justice and fairness. The United States has achieved the first; it only reluctantly gropes toward the second. Yet it must go on groping to fulfill its founding purpose: to increase the sum and improve the conditions of freedom and justice in a world where exhortation and example are not enough. If it is to advance more purposefully and preserve its national integrity in the process, the United States will have to revise the application of some of its inherited values and adapt even more of its institutional procedures to the larger and grosser stage on which it must henceforth succeed or fail. An American imperial polity can accomplish this while remaining democratic at home and without becoming imperialistic abroad. All it has to do is to safeguard at home the conditions of a perpetually controverted and thus dynamic relationship between the people's desires and leadership requirements; and observe abroad the incontrovertible distinction between intervention for police and order and coercion for exploitation and subjection—an observance which will relegate to its proper, formal, plane the now irrelevant distinction between intervention in disturbances within nations and intervention in relations between nations.

There comes a time in the career of nations when to preserve the substance means changing some of the forms; when upholding or revitalizing the mores requires adapting institutional practices and concepts of policy, polity, and popular leadership. The United States may be at such a point; or it may manage, by denying this particular moment's significance, to postpone the maturity of the challenge and thus its own coming of age for one more generation. But, barring a brutal setback of one kind or another, the odds are that this nation will evolve a commitment to a kind of internal and world order which will at once extend and protect its pluralistic society. This is probable. But it is also likely that an imperial polity and policy will emerge into discernible identity only after delays and possible distortions stemming from the misapprehensions and failings of the people, the reformers, and the leaders alike.

For the United States to reduce its international involvement for the sake of domestic peace and justice only to find both eluding it in a constricted and at once contentious and embattled parochial existence would be the supreme irony of American politics. A great power should not incur this risk in a vain quest for immunity from history's tragic dimension. The awe of gods and men is easier to bear than their laughter.